Back to the Cross

Surprising Truths from
Shanghai

For the Chan family.

1 John 3:16

Angela and Ron Oltmanns

&,

The Oltmanns family
Cypress, Tx 2015

Table of Contents

[Preface]   i

Section 1 - Whispers   1

[Chapter 1] Introducing Ron and Angela   1

[Chapter 2] Not just the Memory of Grace   3

[Chapter 3] Life in the Fast Lane   5

Chapter 4] A Heart for the People   8

[Chapter 5] The Road to Shanghai   14

[Chapter 6] Exodus from the US   18

Section 2 – Confronting the Cross   20

[Chapter 7] Warning! Cross Up Ahead   21

[Chapter 8] Losing Titus   28

[Chapter 9] His Word Has Power   32

[Chapter 10] Trying to Nurture Faith   36

[Chapter 11] Starved of the Cross   39

Section 3 – Getting Back to the Cross   42

[Chapter 12] Acts 2 Community   43

[Chapter 13] Living by Faith   50

[Chapter 14] Friends for the Road   54

[Chapter 15] New Eyes to See   57

[Chapter 16] New Attitude at the Office   61

[Chapter 17] A New Look at Work   66

[Chapter 18] Welcoming Help at Home   70

[Chapter 19] A New Look at Healthcare   74

[Chapter 20] A New Look at Real Wealth   77

[Chapter 21] A New Look at Consumption 80

[Chapter 22] Eat Soy Sauce 82

Section 4 – Come Follow Me 84

[Chapter 23] What's Needed? 85

[Chapter 24] Woman at the Well 87

[Chapter 25] Hiddenness 89

[Chapter 26] My Shanghai Knockout Girls 93

[Chapter 27] Not Just "Like": the Cost of Following Christ 99

[Chapter 28] Huang Ayi Teaches Us about Humility 101

[Chapter 29] The Least I Can Do 106

[Chapter 30] On the Road 110

[Chapter 31] Speak Up 113

[Chapter 32] Not Forgotten 116

[Chapter 33] Money and Security 121

[Chapter 34] God's Provision 128

[Chapter 35] Scale a Wall with God 132

[Chapter 36] Hello? Hello! Hello, God. 137

[Chapter 37] Christ Came for the Diors and Chanels Too 140

[Chapter 38] Walking with Our Kids 144

[Chapter 39] Spiritual Amnesia 146

[Chapter 40] Who is My Neighbor? 150

Section 5 – Proclaiming the Cross 155

[Chapter 41] 20 Exits and More 156

[Chapter 42] The Power of One 159

[Chapter 43] Sharing at Frank's 163

[Chapter 44] An Unlikely Friend 165

[Chapter 45] Fellowship 170

[Chapter 46] We Are a New Family 176

[Chapter 47] Time with My Florist 179

[Chapter 48] Family Worship 182

[Chapter 49] Tongues 187

[Chapter 50] Finding God Everywhere:
In the City, In the Village 192

[Chapter 51] Mystery of Christ 197

[Chapter 52] The Church Builds 203

[Chapter 53] The House Church 207

[Chapter 54] Jesus Would Love This Manger! 210

[Chapter 55] Every Tribe, Every Tongue 214

[Chapter 56] Immanuel Became Love 218

Section 6 – What's Next? 221

[Chapter 57] Year of the Snake 222

[Chapter 58] In the Cloud 226

[Chapter 59] Fifteen Minutes or All of Eternal? 229

[Chapter 60] Our Home is Heaven 231

[Chapter 61] Bold New Dreams 235

[Chapter 62] Back to Jerusalem 239

[Chapter 63] Closer, Richer, Deeper 242

[Chapter 64] Landing 246

[Chapter 65] Greater Glory 249

[Chapter 66] What's Next? 252

[Preface]

This book is co-written by two very different people who happen to be married to each other. We could not have lived the experiences we write about without being in a committed relationship, and it has been tried and tested over time.

The message comes in stereo; you will hear some similar things but on two different channels. We have tried to mark who is doing the speaking, but we have not worked overly hard to make it clear each and every time. Angela sounds more conversational and preserves her sentence fragments—it's her style. Ron focuses on ideas and likes to leave the reader with something to ponder.

This book is written for those who follow Christ. If you have been a Christian for a while and your faith feels more like dry duty than loving devotion, more frenzied hurry than sweet pleasure or if you are just struggling to keep faith, please read on.

This book is also written for those who are interested in Jesus or who have looked at some parts of the Bible. You are attracted to Jesus or his message but for your own reasons have not made a full commitment to follow Christ. Perhaps you can gain from our experience and stories.

The main message of this book is that even for those who have chosen to follow Christ, the daily decisions and weekly rituals and yearly passage of time require us to look closely and truthfully at the question: are we really following Him or have we diverted after someone or something else? The Christian life is based on the claim that God is the higher authority and His way is taught and demonstrated most clearly and perfectly in Jesus Christ; we should be following *Him*.

Following Christ will involve challenge, sometimes hardship and unexpected developments. A short way to say it is this: Following Christ must go the way of the cross. A Christian life without the cross is really just a cultural substitute, not the path Jesus called people to walk.

We want to share with you how we have grown to this realization over the last several years when our family decided with some faith and courage to leap into the arms of God and say "yes" to a move to China. It was in China that we found ourselves drawn deeper into what a missional life would look like. In the process we discovered surprising truths about ourselves, the people we came into contact with and God Himself – who He really is.

Most of this book was written "in the moment" while we were in China. The present tense captures the immediacy of the moment. We have also reflected on these stories and experiences, so sometimes the past tense comes in. We decided not to smooth this out and make it uniform even though our English teachers might not fully approve. In the end we are not trying to write great literature; we are aiming to speak to the heart.

We hope through the stories we share, you'll be encouraged to take another look at the cross, and see these words from Jesus in a completely new light.

"I have come that they may have life, and have it to the full." John 10:10

If you gain some insight or find motivation to take an action, that is our intent and we will be so happy for you to have life to the full.

Section 1 - Whispers

[Chapter 1] Introducing Ron and Angela

/Angela/ In 1989, I met a boy. He said he heard my voice first. It was that voice that made an impression. For me, it was his face, by the door, as he ushered guests into the church. Serious. Handsome. Present. I stopped to look and noticed a godly soul.

It was a good summer for me that year. We learned more about the Good News together. We shared stories of our families, our faith, what it is like to follow Christ.

What I didn't expect was that I would marry that boy. I admire Ron about many things but there were also many things we did not appreciate from the same angle. In so many ways my relationship with him mirrored my other relationships in life. It is not always about getting on the same page but always an opportunity from God to help me understand what a full life with Christ means.

\Ron\ I was born in Venezuela and grew up in the US. I became a Christian when I was young and despite some missteps in the early years, I committed myself to this path in the middle of my teenage years and before I left home, I had already ventured to Brazil and caught a bigger picture of God's working in this world.

When I met Angela in 1989, I had a clear sense that I was going to make my life matter for God. As I traveled around Southeast Asia that summer to Thailand, Malaysia, Indonesia and Singapore, I was looking for signs of what God wanted from me. At the same time, things were moving in the world. Walls were coming down in Eastern Europe while China was rocked by Tiananmen. I met Angela and we talked about things large and small as a friendship developed.

I didn't expect at the time that after graduate school I would end up living in Singapore for five years, or that Angela and I would be married. We ended up settling in the US over the next sixteen years and added two boys to our family. I couldn't foresee that 22 years after Angela and I met that we would together move with our two boys to live in China as part of living out our life purpose.

[Chapter 2] Not just the Memory of Grace

\Ron\ "Help us see the gospel afresh every day, to live out the gospel and experience its freshness and power. Let us live in the abundance of God's grace daily and *not just the memory of grace*" - (April 12, 2011)

/Angela/ I was baptized in 1988 while I was in junior college. My whole life lay ahead of me, waiting to be explored and discovered. And I said "yes" to God, against the wishes of my mother. As much as my society had prepared me for a successful life, I knew for my adventure ahead, I needed unprecedented strength, divine wisdom and uncommon courage. That comes from a source above.

My parents had given me their example of indomitable spirit and sacrifice. My father left his family and Communist China as a young lad in the 1940's. He struck out boldly into the world to learn a trade and make a good living for his family. It led him to Hong Kong, then to Singapore where he met my mother and we lived in Indonesia for a while. In the end, he faced a terminal disease that ended his life just before I turned 11. My mother, widowed when she was 32, raised the two of us, my younger brother and I, as a s ngle parent. She was a loyal woman, full of diligence and gave her best self to work. I admire her resolution in getting things done.

Against this semi-Confucian background, I was however gripped by an unexplainable tug to follow God even though my family objected to it. My father's disapproval restrained my faith search. But God knocked on my door through various people throughout my high school years. In the end, I decided that I would follow Christ. In spite of my gregarious personality, I was however still too nervous and shy for public acknowledgment to be baptized before the Sunday crowd. So I called up my pastor, Charlie, and ask if he could baptize me on a weekday.

And so it happened, that particular Wednesday in December, I got into the bathtub at church for my water baptism. With just Joysia, Charlie, my pastor and a boy whose name I no longer remember, I let myself be immersed and come up anew.

Yet with all the thousands of sermons I heard, small group fellowships I attended and acts of kindness I have done, I thought my faith journey would just be one continuous upward move toward holiness. Instead, in the midst of some very missional living in China, I found myself writing this journal entry.

January 2012

Romans 8:28 "My struggle is – Really, is it really true? I often do not believe that God works toward the good of me who love Him. If He does, my life would be smooth-sailing, easy and happy. I have to trust that God really does work toward the good of me who love Him."

So do I still believe in the Power of the Cross? Oh yes, I do. Therein lies the paradox.

"For the measure of the cross is foolishness to those who are perishing, but to us who are being saved it is the power of God." 1 Corinthians 1:18

4

[Chapter 3] Life in the Fast Lane

"I wanted to see what was worthwhile for men to do under heaven during the few days of their lives. I undertook great projects: I built houses for myself and planted vineyards. I amassed silver and gold for myself, and the treasure of kings and provinces." Ecclesiastes 2:3b,4,8

\Ron\ We spent over ten years living near Dallas-Ft. Worth, Texas, from 1999 and we originally moved there looking for more business opportunities. We lived in the near suburb of Irving at first, then when our second son came less than two years after our first, we moved up to Denton. Our intention was to raise our family out of the city in an affordable community, to live modestly. Church was important to us and we always sought to worship with a community that would help us grow our faith. Before children we were pretty active in our church, but after two boys came we were less so. We worshipped every week and we took our faith seriously, but we were not actively giving back through the church.

My time and attention was very much on growing my career and business. Angela was fully immersed in the duties of raising babies. We prospered and enjoyed years of plenty. I traveled a lot for my work, yet I thought I was very involved as a parent. At times we would wonder to ourselves, "Should we be living somewhere else? Should we be pursuing another kind of life?" The thought of packing up and traveling around the world for a year with the family was an enticing fantasy for us.

To work and serve others in another country with young children in tow seemed an even more fantastical idea. We reasoned that we would have to already have a substantial amount saved and be financially independent. We weren't there yet, but still we experimented with the possibility through a few trips to Mexico. Of course we would carry our faith with us, but it wasn't really the primary thing driving us. Our own agenda and desires were at the center. Instead of going we gave to others who went overseas to serve.

In 2010 we planned a trip back to Singapore to visit Angela's family. Our boys had only been there once before, almost too young to remember much, and we wanted them to have the chance to renew ties with that side of their family. As we got into planning the details, we found ourselves by God's wisdom routed through China on the way to Singapore.

We knew a few friends who were in China and thought maybe we could spend some time there as a family. The World Expo was also going on that year in Shanghai, and we were eager to expose our boys to a window on the wider world. Honestly, *I* was keenly interested in seeing China since the last time I had been there in 1992 on a brief trip to the southern city of Guangzhou. Truth be told, Angela probably would have preferred going to Europe instead of China, but she put the family first as we set off on our three week's trip to Asia.

Shanghai, China – Expo 2010

Our first peek at Shanghai after a long flight revealed a large, built-up city with dense office buildings and tall apartment towers. We settled near Renmin Park in the middle of the city and met a group of elderly Shanghai people out for their morning exercise on our first morning after waking up in China. "We came for the Expo" we told them. They were friendly toward us and pleased to see our efforts to communicate with them in Chinese. We finally said good bye with "zei wei".

A good friend of ours had moved to Shanghai and had a small rented apartment in Xuhui. She was not in town, but she offered to let us stay at her place during our time there. So after a few days we moved from the hotel to the local apartment in a neighborhood that seemed a little further out from the city center. The studio apartment had the advantages of a small kitchen we would cook in and a washing machine to do our laundry. It was also economical. It put us in close quarters, however, and it required us to adjust to living a little more like locals, buying food in the fresh market, getting supplies for the house at the local supermarket.

We enjoyed our time in Shanghai, taking in the Expo, meeting up with some of Angela's old school friends from Singapore who were living in Shanghai, going to a water town near Shanghai, attending worship at Shanghai Community Fellowship, the international church on Hengshan Road. I also went to meet with some potential business partners on one morning. We felt like we were getting a full immersion experience in China in spite of the sweltering summer heat and great crowds.

We went to Singapore and spent time with Angela's family. We returned through Shanghai a second time, but we only had two days and we stayed at a hotel in Pudong near Century Park. With 24 million people it has five times Singapore's population. Looking back now, I saw it through foreign, uncomprehending eyes. We could only see the surface of things. It was only with time that we would be initiated to see things on a wholly different level.

Chapter 4] A Heart for the People

"While Paul was waiting for them in Athens, he was greatly distressed to see that the city was full of idols. So he reasoned in the synagogue with both Jews and God-fearing Greeks, as well as in the marketplace day by day with those who happened to be there.

Paul then stood up in the meeting of the Areopagus and said: "People of Athens! I see that in every way you are very religious. For as I walked around and looked carefully at your objects of worship, I even found an altar with this inscription: to an unknown god. So you are ignorant of the very thing you worship—and this is what I am going to proclaim to you. The God who made the world and everything in it is the Lord of heaven and earth and does not live in temples built by human hands. " Acts 17:16-17, 22-24.

/Angela/ It was a cool summer night in 2010 when I first set foot on the Nanjing Lu Pedestrian Walk (南京步行街). By the steps where the underground tunnel led to the Line 2 subway, I found myself a great vantage point to people watch. I stood there, mesmerized. My Chinese ears made out a variety of provincial dialects from the domestic tourists. The faces were all Chinese but they spoke different languages. The sheer diversity heard that night convinced me once more that this truly was a nation of over a billion people. On that night, a few German and Russian tourists also stood out. Apparently everyone was excited about the city of Shanghai.

Everyone had one singular purpose: to take as many pictures possible, from every angle, all to remember their magical night here. For these tourists near and far, Shanghai definitely delivered the glitter and the awe. I too was thrilled to be here.

I wanted a moment to experience this city alone. So, Ron took the boys back to the J W Marriott, just a stone's throw away at Tomorrow Square. Coming up from the subway, I was greeted by a magnificent display of neon lights and attention-grabbing advertisements. The messages were all in Chinese and they captured in brief the dynamism and commercial might of this city.

Shanghai was a detour we didn't intend. In the summer of 2010, our family of four was headed for a family visit to Singapore. Several things happened and we found ourselves on an extended stopover in Shanghai.

"What do you do in Shanghai?" I asked my husband, Ron.

"Well, they are having the World Expo there this year," he offered.

City travel in my view was not so fun for young children. Turning it into an educational tour with a glimpse of this former Paris of the East, even in the heat of summer had its attractive s de. So, off we went. What I thought would be a fun cultural learning trip for the boys became a trip for Goc to speak more deeply into my faith journey with Him.

To be sure, I am Chinese, but as one born and raised overseas (outside China), it was my past, not much different from how many Americans see their European heritage. Yet strangely that night, with a well laid suburban American life waiting for me back home, I found myself overcome with a deep sense of compassion for this sea of humanity, all no relation to me.

Is that how Jesus felt when he looked over Jerusalem? (Luke 19:41)

The words by the apostle Paul in Acts 17 rang in my head as I imagined him on Mars Hill, preaching to the Greeks. I was no spiritual giant, definitely not a Paul, not even a missionary commissioned by the church. What then was my place in sharing the Good News with others? I was disturbed that other than the occasional good deeds I did and the programs I participated in at church, I had no clear missional plan.

That night, the endless wave of humanity served me as a strong visual reminder. Their constant coming and going from one end of the pedestrian walk to the other reminded me just how big the world was and how disengaged I had been with it.

Who would tell them about Jesus? Did they even need to know?

I was full of emotions inside. My heart ached heavy. I was also a little confused. I became sorely aware of how little I knew about God's power at work, no different from all the foreign faces around me. Was I also just like them? Distracted by the surface? All I knew was I could not return to worshipping God in my comfortable American church in the same fashion I did before. Almost two decades of it was quite enough. But what was to change?

It was one night that year late in the fall after our tourist trip to China when I heard His voice clear as a Macedonian clarion call. The instruction was simple, "**Go** to China, but **not** now." I awoke from my sleep, unused to hearing such plain, explicit instruction from the Holy. I remember keeping it in my heart for days,

10

continuing my usual slow meditative walks in my neighborhood. I stared at the pavement as I walked and found myself paying closer attention all around. Maybe it really was time to close a chapter here. The boys soon returned to another year at Coram Deo Academy in Flower Mound, Texas.

Fall soon came and the change in weather brought in a new season of reflection.

There was nothing spectacular in the way courage and faith were slowly sown into my heart. In my journal entries then, I was still an anxious parent, often on my knees in prayer how to work with my children. Help me be sensitive to the sins in my life I would write. Help me be sensitive to the consequences of my sins on others. Help me, I would plea further, be compassionate for others. And finally, it was, "Lord, help me obey your commands." Little did I know, some of these prayers would actually take the passing of many seasons before I saw them answered.

October 2010 Journal Entry

"I ask that I remain steadfast in my homeschooling/Coram Deo work. Lord, I'm not sure if it's 2011 or 2012 or 2015 or 2020 that we're to go to China to serve. But I trust that you'll tell me. In the meantime, thank you for the chance to grow and learn here. They seem like such minor things- learning to sew, getting along, helping the people here; teaching these two very active and strong-willed boys but I pray lord you'll not forsake me. Show me mercy. Help me do my job well here so that I may have courage and confidence to do even bigger jobs for You later. In Jesus' name, I pray and ask, Amen."

11

In early December, I received word that the boys needed to declare and ask Jesus to be the Lord of their lives as our next steps to China. Our older son, Markus, was ready and we soon scheduled to have his baptism be held at the church in Houston where his grandparents attend.

Even as we anchored ourselves to live more missionally, the skill and spirit to become one mind with Christ came about slowly. I whined a great deal, I was upset constantly and I even cursed God! There were a lot of uncertainties and I did not appreciate stepping out under those terms.

January 2011 Journal Entry

"Dear God, I continue to pray and seek your prayers on our China move. When? How? Where (to live?) Do I go over Spring break to recce? Lord, please continue to show signs. My dreams tell me that it's a new territory, fraught with dangers (so, be careful). Do I not know that already? Then Lord, why ask me to set sail on treacherous waters? Isn't the calm dock fine?"

There is something about a Holy God, ever constant and never changing in His patient love. Eventually, such love quiets even the most distraught child like me.

It also became obvious to me that while I could insist on many things with my children, I could not demand their affection for my God. I needed to do some changing myself, and that was the hard part. My second son, Titus, did in fact make his own decision just before our departure. In August, the same day his father was baptized some 32 years ago, Titus said "Yes" to God. I felt our family was united spiritually but also not quite ready for the new chapter ahead.

[Chapter 5] The Road to Shanghai

"Do not be afraid or discouraged because of this vast army. For the battle is not yours but God's...Go out to face them tomorrow and the Lord will be with you."

2 Chronicles 20:15,17

\Ron\ Radical moves always look more romantic from the sidelines. When you are in the middle of them, all you know is that life is coming at you fast and you have to do *something*.

People who don't know us well might look at us and think "Of course you moved to China. It makes perfect sense!" But it didn't look that way to us.

Angela was born and raised in Singapore in an ethnic Chinese family. She spoke Mandarin from young in her home, so many people assume it is natural for her to come to China. The truth is that there was little interest on her part to come. As you just read, once she was here God pricked her heart and gave her great empathy for the people of China, but it was not really there before that trip.

I didn't grow up with a fascination about China. I've always had more interest drawing me back to South America. I did live in Singapore in the early 90's and traveled in Asia, including southern China a few times, before moving back to the US in 1995. As the reform and opening in China started to take off I considered moving to China, but it never got beyond an idea.

I started learning Mandarin Chinese in 1990 even before I moved to Singapore. A graduate student from Beijing was attending my university and she gave me private lessons. When I lived in Singapore I had one year of formal language instruction at the National

University of Singapore and then I just kept learning on my own over the years, sometimes more earnestly and sometimes neglecting it almost completely. At least some of it seems to have stuck. God can use just about anything for his purposes when we decide to align with him.

There were a few times that I wondered if I would ever make a trip to China or even live there at some time in the future, but things never seemed to come together. A friend in business started telling me in 2007 about his son living in China and his own business interest there. It raised my attention, but it took several years and our family trip to visit the 2010 Expo in Shanghai before the pieces started coming together.

When we returned from our summer trip in 2010, we were astounded to hear at our church that the founder and senior pastor had announced while we were gone that he and his family were going to be making a transition over the next year, leaving this thriving church of several thousand in North Texas that they had planted 18 years earlier, and moving to China to do leadership development.

Some people would say that was quite a coincidence. As believers in a powerful and unpredictable God, we saw more than coincidence. It got our attention. Over the next several weeks, we had to look at our own lives and willingness to do something as bold as this pastor and his family were undertaking.

In our first few months in Shanghai we were asked many times the same question, phrased a few different ways, "Why did you come to China?" People usually were not asking for a full explanation, they were just curious and wanted a short answer for their curiosity.

15

How we answer questions like this tells other people something about us, who we are. Common answers: I came to China to make money; I came to live in another culture; I came to see another part of the world; and much less commonly, I came to make a difference in the world. You can hear all of these in the stories of other expatriates in China, and each of those answers has some truth in it for us.

The short and most direct answer to the question goes something like this. In one conversation several weeks after we arrived in China, Chris, a pastor's wife in Shanghai, asked us a typical newcomer's question that stumped us at first.

"Who sent you here?" she asked with great warmth and interest, since many in the congregation were expatriates sent here by companies. The typical answer was the name of the sponsoring company, but we didn't fit that. I was hardly ever stumped for an answer but this time I was. Suddenly I found myself saying, with joy and life in my voice, "No one, God did!" The three of us broke out into happy laughter and smiles. Yes, God sent all of us here.

We put prayer into this decision and strikingly we got clear answers. God made it clear he wanted us in China. We had other circumstantial reasons for our move: we wanted to make money and China's economy was doing better than the West, especially after 2008. There were business opportunities here, and we wanted to also expose our boys to another culture and help them learn another language before they turned ten.

At the same time, there would be sacrifices. For all of us, it would mean much greater distance and less time spent with my family in Texas. For our boys, they would miss their friends at school and a great martial arts program that they belonged to. Angela would give up the comforts of our home and familiar routines for something unknown and probably difficult at times.

In November 2010 I returned to China to do some training on behalf of a small consulting firm in Shanghai for a large corporate client. In subsequent months they had some potential big projects and also some internal needs for staff development. They asked me to consider stepping in to help. This led to me making a series of trips over the next months to spend a week or two in China.

By springtime 2011, it seemed increasingly possible and even likely that we would move to China. We prepared to break the news to family and friends, to put our house on the market, to prepare ourselves for what lay ahead. There were uncertainties about some of the details (our house didn't sell in a sluggish housing market, our partnership with the firm in China was more informal than formally detailed, we had some personal debt we still wanted to clear), but we felt a strong sense of calling to go.

[Chapter 6] Exodus from the US

/Angela/ In the last days before our departure, many things were still undecided. And everything required accounting for. For instance, what would we do with our vehicles? It was easy to sell our new Toyota Camry Hybrid. The dealership which we bought it from was just five minutes from our house. But what about our Toyota Sienna minivan, already getting along in years? We decided to keep it until the day we left and then donate it to our Aikido instructor who was a big help to us.

Although we had intentionally chosen to live simply, we still had much to either dispose of or store away. A mother and her teenage son came over to help. What a blessing! Those who couldn't come over did other things. Two moms got together and took our boys swimming. Another delivered a roast. The greeter who had given us unfailing hello's weekly at the church entrance became the real estate agent we needed to list our house. In spite of all this generous goodwill, we felt great loneliness inside about our mission.

We had left places before and in each farewell, there was often a season of general fanfare for us and goodbyes. Usually there was a spirit of great optimism about something brighter to come. In one, we had a plaque made out for us and a huge sendoff at the airport. In another, we even had time to reminisce good memories made over several wonderful dinners.

This time, however, things were a little quiet. We were eager for the new chapter but we also felt nervous about what may lay ahead. Perhaps that was the only way the wings of angels could come and spread themselves to lift us off to China.

Lest there be any grand illusions about it, the journey was stressful from the start. The night before our flight it felt like the exodus from Egypt. Ron was packing up last minute things and I was not at peace. What were we to do? In one of my insane moments, I wanted to bail out and not go. God heard it all.

A long-time business colleague of ours is a Mormon and mentioned that two elders from a nearby ward could come help us, so two complete strangers came to help us move heavy boxes into our storage unit. Even in the final moments of our big move, God had begun His lesson. My world is bigger than you think, He said.

On the morning of our flight, the airline agent held us up because of a question about our two boys' visas to China. It was nerve-wracking and almost made us miss our flight, but finally we got on the plane and left home. We finally made our extraordinary exodus from Texas in a most nondescript fashion. A few flight stewardesses found out that we were actually heading to China to live. Midway on that flight, they surprised us with a classy bottle of champagne. It felt odd to be celebrated this way but God would have none of our anxieties. Come journey and celebrate this new path!

Section 2 – Confronting the Cross

[Chapter 7] Warning! Cross Up Ahead

\Ron\ We landed in Shanghai in the middle of August 2011. Angela's mom had helped us pack up our things in the US and she traveled with us for our first few weeks in China. We stayed for two weeks in a temporary serviced apartment. We set about house-hunting and getting the boys enrolled in a school while we celebrated our oldest son Markus's ninth birthday.

We decided to put our boys in the international division of a bilingual school in Pudong called Pinghe. After looking at many properties and praying fervently for the right decision, we decided on a two bedroom apartment in Lujiazui, the downtown financial district. We had about half the space of our house in the US, a small kitchen, and our boys shared a bedroom.

Dealing with a real estate agent and landlord and negotiating the move-in details took a lot of energy. As newcomers we realized we were in the dark about how things worked, what we could ask for, how to negotiate and how hard to push, what is a good deal—for all of this we lacked adequate guidance, so we tried to do the reasonable thing and not worry too much about how smart we were being.

The boys started school in September and had to ride a school bus at 7am and they got home around 5pm. They were pretty tired when they got home. I started going into the office and adjusting to the working demands of the business culture in Shanghai. There were a lot of client visits and learning to work with our local office staff and colleagues.

21

We had bright spots of course. Our boys were in a good school and learning Chinese. We found a church quickly and started a home group meeting in our apartment with the support of an elder from church. Angela had some school friends from Singapore who had lived in China several years and were already well-adjusted and very helpful and understanding toward us.

But after that first month the difficulties came. Here is something I wrote then that captures the flavor of what we were facing early on.

"We are 8,000 miles from home, separated by a vast ocean and our plumbing has failed...again. Our base salary at the local company I work for got dropped and we don't know three months from now where our boys will go to school, or how we'll be paying rent.

"We came to Shanghai, China, for work and to save a bundle as much as anything. We wanted to give our boys a chance to learn a new language and culture. We were so sure that God was in this, that he wanted us to be here at this time. Where is God now in all of this?

"We moved to China three months ago. It takes great effort to get things done, to communicate with taxi drivers, to negotiate with the landlord for a new mattress or lighting to lighten up our dark apartment, to learn where to buy food (there's no one-stop place to get everything we need), to deal with sickness in the family and lack of appetite, and amidst all of this to answer the big question: what are we doing here? What role are we supposed to play? God, *why* did you bring us here?"

We did not consider ourselves missionaries. We were just an ordinary family. We didn't sign up for a hardship posting. The people we left behind in the US thought we were setting off on a grand adventure. This adventure has no romance in it anymore. It's just hard. Discouragement tails us doggedly.

"The Son of Man must suffer many things and be rejected by the elders, the chief priests and teachers of the law, and he must be killed and on the third day be raised to life."

Then he said to them all: "If anyone would come after me, he must deny himself and take up his cross daily and follow me." Luke 9:22-23

For Jesus' first disciples, this was a stark warning. Up to this point there had been miracles and healing and gracious teaching. There were questions and opposition, there was misunderstanding too, but up to this point following Jesus was an adventure. He was a popular teacher who was becoming known in Palestine. He put his followers on notice: there is a cross up ahead. If you stay on this path, it will include suffering and rejection and death, and not just for me alone. Anyone who follows me is taking on a life lived daily in the shadow of the cross.

When our family moved to China, a close friend of mine counseled me that with such a major move and life change, it would probably take six months to re-wire the brain, for all the neural pathways to make the adjustment to our new environment and the realities of what was going on. I recalled his words a number of times, and it certainly took that long to re-route the body's plumbing!

All four of us got physically sick after about a month in Shanghai adjusting to new food, water and the general environment. The Chinese have an expression for this "shui tu bu fu" (水土不服) – not matched to the water and soil (of a strange place). Some adjust quickly, some never make the changeover. It took us a while to get adjusted. My wife Angela lost her appetite and went several months eating very meager meals. We also sought various help to treat the boys' incessant coughs. It was discouraging at the time, but I've come to see it's just the reality of international moves and a change of lifestyle. Dealing with changes was one difficult lesson but doubting the power of the cross was more difficult to bear.

My work situation too became less stable and predictable soon after we arrived. The partners in the small firm I joined had a major difference and eventually separated. We moved into new, smaller offices two months after I arrived. The amount of client work I expected didn't materialize. I had to consider other work options to plan for a worst case scenario of unemployment

In all of these events, I was being warned, "There is a cross up ahead." But I tried to look on the bright side and rationalize what was happening or would happen. Asking why we landed in this situation didn't seem to be the right thing. We had to also ask, "God, did we understand the signs right? Were we really supposed to move here? Why are we here anyway?" We didn't get immediate answers to the questions, but we started listening more intently for answers, even the ones that didn't match our understanding. Training ourselves to listen beyond the surface required both heart and wisdom from above.

/Angela/ 别担心。"Don't worry."

我们不会骗你的。"We won't cheat you."

I heard these two lines frequently when I interacted with the locals. To be sure, I had paid bills and interfaced with different people before but to do it in a new country albeit in a language familiar to me required a new facility from me. Most times in the beginning, it was both stressful and not smooth-sailing at all. The Chinese had their own way of making sense of their things. I was passed around person to person. They spoke Shanghainese to one another. Counter to counter, person to person, I was moved around in a long human chain of people. Total bewilderment didn't help one bit.

Many times I had to focus my eyes on the cross to get things done. Anything else would have derailed the tasks at hand that needed my attention. Renting an apartment, working with Chinese real estate agents, paying the bills, using their banking system, dealing with delivery people, getting parts for leaky plumbing and dealing with repairmen, buying food in the markets, finding what we needed either at stores or online, learning the transportation system which includes the bus, subway, taxi, inter-city train and ferry—could leave one's nerves strained and dispirited. But God was enough. The more depleted I was, the more I didn't know how to function on my own strengths and smarts, the more God was able to fill me up with His solutions and perspectives.

/Ron/ One of the lessons learned from this season is that obedience is non-negotiable, while understanding is optional. It is tempting to delay our obedience to God until we really understand the situation or think we know what is going on. There is something in scripture we need to obey, or a prompting from the Spirit, or an obvious discipline is laid upon us. At these times, do we obey quickly and willingly, or do we put it off because we object, or don't think it's fair, or don't even see the reason behind it?

I have seen this same lesson with my two boys. I ask them to do something that is reasonable and even beneficial to them. Explaining "why" to them doesn't always result in obedience. It doesn't even guarantee that they understand. But what really matters anyway is obedience. Often it is only *after* we have obeyed and demonstrated faithfulness that we are given the chance to understand why it was necessary or how it makes sense.

The cross does not make sense. The apostle Paul wrote in 1 Corinthians 1 that the message of the cross is foolish to the world's way of thinking. The flesh resists the way of the cross; the cross makes no earthly sense. I think Jesus in full humanity and full deity also wrestled with it.

From the human side, the cross is not only illogical, it also appears cruel and unnecessary. From the divine side, seen through love, there is simply no other way.

There is a very interesting verse in the book of Hebrews about this.

> *"During the days of Jesus' life on earth, he offered up prayers and petitions with loud cries and tears to the one who could save him from death, and he was heard because of his reverent submission. Although he was a son, he learned obedience from what he suffered..."* Hebrews 5:7-8

For me and my family, we didn't realize that we were being led deeper into a fellowship with Christ and

26

his cross. Signs and warnings were there, but we just couldn't see them or even comprehend that this was the way for us to walk. This makes me wonder: how often have we missed the way of the cross because we weren't expecting it, we rationalized an easier way for ourselves, or we simply didn't submit ourselves to obedience before we fully understood why it was necessary?

[Chapter 8] Losing Titus

"My prayer is not that you take them out of the world but you protect them from the evil one." John 17:15

/Angela/ "Su, I lost Titus! I am buying shampoo here at Jia De Li. The next moment, Titus is GONE! He is not at the store. Not out on the street. Not anywhere. I have no idea where he is!" I gushed out the second Susan, a high school friend I reconnected with in Shanghai, picked up my call.

"OK!" responded Susan quickly back. Having a young son herself, she understood my panic right away. "Eric and I are coming."

Barely two weeks into the city, and I had lost my seven year old son. The shining lights of Shanghai's financial center lit up our Lujiazui district, a cold landscape of glitter without heart. Before me, PuCheng Lu continued onward from downtown into new territory still foreign to me. If I walked toward the right, I would hit the landmark Huangpu River that divides the city from the old city of Puxi and the dynamic development of Pudong.   Surely he wouldn't have made a left? One finds the metro station there but we haven't even learned how to use the transport system yet.

I suddenly felt like Abraham at Mount Moriah with his son, Isaac. I trust my God but to offer up my son lost into the darkness of China seemed like one cruel sacrifice to me.

We had told the boys many times not to go off alone or leave our sight. I had not established a routine for my shopping or yet discovered where to find everything we needed. We had heard the stories about

28

missing children. What could have happened to Titus? Ron ran from the small grocery store we had been shopping in toward our apartment about ten minutes away.

I screamed Titus's name on the busy street. A young man, soliciting sales for his real estate company on the sidewalk, stopped handing out flyers and joined me in my concern. I screamed for his name again, losing hope like sand slipping through an hourglass. My Titanic was sinking fast.

Could he hear my voice above the din of city traffic noise? I stood frozen in devastation at the corner of Shangcheng Lu and Pucheng Lu. Nothing I had or possessed could help me find Titus. Fear gripped me like a crazy dog. The first few lines from Yeats' poem, *The Second Coming,* came to me nonstop.

"The center cannot hold. The center cannot hold." Like the falcon who cannot hear the falconer, I could not hear my God.

"Oh Lord, save me, please," I pleaded. "Save us, please, "I prayed and would not let go that line.

While I stood waiting for Titus to be returned to me, Ron called to my relief that he had found Titus at our apartment, shaken and crying. How he managed those busy streets without experience, three city blocks and traffic lights, and crossed them himself still amazes me to this very day. Against any of my expectations, he had found his way home, thanks to the Father from above.

I called Susan up and shared the news. She was also knotted up like I was. "Are you sure you don't need us? Eric and I are in our car now," she said.

"No, we're ok now. Thanks for wanting to come. Enjoy the rest of the night," I replied.

In time, I was able to recount that terrifying story with both humor and lightness with family and friends. But inside, something else was birthing forth. It seemed a new center was emerging and I could feel the old crusts of self forced to make way for a new self. Even without a burning bush appearance, it seemed God was already present, helping me see that with Him, indeed all things are made new (2 Corinthians 5:17).

I had thought perhaps all my major testing was done when I decided to follow Christ years back. Who knew that more tests of faith would continue to unfold as the years roll on and my children's feet become larger than my own? Maybe we are all to be like Abraham in some aspect, even at seventy-five, was willing to be called and go.

God in His good wisdom established quickly His sovereignty in our lives even before we could find the right shampoo in China. He gave my son a homing instinct in a city that wasn't familiar to him. By allowing such heart-stopping fright and fast thanksgiving so early on in our experience, I believe He was in fact saying, "That's right. You can't cage him but I will look out for you."

And that is the truth I had to yield to in spite of my disbelieving mind. The fear would always be there: of losing something precious to me, of being hurt so badly that I didn't think I could ever bear it. But trust we must, in the face of this almost unendurable feeling and thinking that we had lost our center.

If there is any first lesson to learn newly about the Cross, it would be this: The Lord has our backs.

Surely goodness and love will follow us all the days of our lives. (Psalms 23:6)

[Chapter 9] His Word Has Power

"Jesus asked him, "What is your name?"
"Legion," he replied, because many demons had gone into him.
And they begged Jesus repeatedly not to order them to go into
the Abyss. A large herd of pigs was feeding there on the
hillside. The demons begged Jesus to let them go into the pigs,
and he gave them permission. When the demons came out of
the man, they went into the pigs, and the herd rushed down the
steep bank into the lake and was drowned. Luke 8:30-33."

/Angela/ A few months after I arrived into the city of Shanghai, feeling brave, I took the subway and ventured from Pudong to Puxi, two stops from where I lived, and decided to meet my husband there for lunch.

While waiting for him at the food court, a young woman with an odd aura about her sat herself down at my table. There were several empty tables around me, so I wasn't sure what to make of her, was she audacious or intense, or something else? I could leave, I thought, and let her have my table since I was still feeling like a fish out of water, and I had no forthrightness that moment to ask her to leave.

妇人，你要算命吗？"Would you like me to read your fortune, ma'am?" she asked politely.

Immediately, my discomfort switched to annoyance. Did I really look like an easy target for such things?

没关系。我不算你钱．"No worries. I will not charge you," she continued.

Now, I must confess that once upon a time, even the churchgoer that I am, I would have said yes.

Especially when I know my husband is arriving in a few minutes and being the black belt that he is, I would essentially have nothing to fear.

But there is something about being further along the road, years of deeper understanding of the Word that I become aware that spiritual forces at work around us are not to be dabbled with. Earlier in life I would have indulged my curiosity and thought of it as a tame form of innocent entertainment. Today, I don't want to get mixed up with such things.

Moreover, and seriously, didn't we come to Shanghai for God?

Firmly, I said, "不，谢了." Basically, "No, thank you."

Ron shortly arrived and realizing I had reinforcements and was not a one, she stopped her pleas and left.

Although I wasn't harmed in anyway, I couldn't help but feel disturbed.

"I need to be on my guard,' I thought out loud as I dug into the food Ron got us.

Ron agreed. "Tell her that you've got Jesus."

My face wrinkled up. Huh? "Oh yeah, right," I replied. We continued eating our lunch, delighted that we had a couple of moments together. We soon parted ways and with an hour to spare, I decided I would check out the mall, Raffles City Shanghai. It was a development by Singaporeans, people from my home country, so I was curious to see what is was like.

So off I went. I proceeded floor by floor using the escalators. It had an open center with six or seven flights of escalators like many Asian shopping malls. My attention was on the window displays of the retail stores.

Shanghai is no small town. In fact, it is the largest city proper in the world. Every day, the same spot changes its scenery. Who you see and meet today, you may likely never encounter again. That is how big the city of 24 million people is.

Or so I thought.

But right at the 6th floor, just as I was going down the escalator, the same lady who wanted to read my fortune a moment ago met me again. She wanted to be my friend. I desperately wanted to shake off the dark shimmies she seemed to be bringing my way. I refused all advances of her friendship. I know, not a very Christ-like attitude, but I didn't feel very safe either. I was a newcomer in a strange land.

我不信佛。我是跟耶稣的. "I do not worship Buddha. I follow Jesus," I finally said to her as she followed me.

All of a sudden, she started sharing and preaching. Delighted that I had a spiritual path myself, she wanted to tell me how Buddhism had saved her. I knew just enough stories from personal study and growing up in a Buddhist/Taoist family and having friends who believed that I could ask this question, "So, you are doing this to redeem yourself? To do good and earn some merit?"

She said yes.

Our eyes met. My judgment fell away.

"I have done too much wrong. This is my way to express gratitude," she said softly, "Let me tell your fortune, please."

I don't need this woman to read my fortune but how do I answer her?

Then Jesus said to her, "Your sins are forgiven." Luke 7:48

That verse, heard more times than I can remember from the pulpit, just stumbled out from my mouth. As soon as I said that, her countenance changed. Tears started to well up in her eyes.

你不需这样做。耶稣已洗了你的罪. "You don't have to do this," I said. "Christ has redeemed you and forgiven you for it."

I am not sure if those words made any sense to her. But she just stopped. I would like to think she understood me. I no longer was pursued and she let me go.

I eventually found my subway home, again amazed at the truth and power of Jesus' words. God's Word had found its mark, and even now I am amazed that God had set up that appointment, this connection so that this woman could hear what He wanted to say to her.

"Your sins are forgiven."

His word truly has power.

[Chapter 10] Trying to Nurture Faith

"So, just as you received Christ Jesus as Lord, keep walking in him, rooted and built up in him, strengthened in the faith just as you were taught, and overflowing with thankfulness."
Colossians 2:6-7

\Ron\ Before we left the US I spent the first half of 2011 pondering how to be rooted in the Christian faith, how to have deep roots and not easily be shaken. I needed it for myself, and I wanted to lead our family spiritually. My two sons were both new young believers, and as a family we would all need to stay rooted in what was important as we plunged ahead into a new culture and a completely different setting from where we had been comfortably nestled the las ten years.

I spent time in the short letter to the Colossians, meditating on its message. When we arrived in Shanghai, I went onto its close cousin, the letter to the Ephesians. When we started a home group in our apartment in September, we used the Ephesian letter as our study material.

The word of God is essential for living the Christian life. It is not necessary to be or become a Bible scholar, but getting fully familiar with God's word and using it to launch us in prayer, to provide guidance for our everyday decisions—these *are* necessary in order to grow in the faith. The other necessary thing is putting God's truth into practice! God tells us to love our neighbor; do I show love for my neighbors in practical ways? God shows us mercy, kindness and patience; am I growing in mercy, kindness and patience?

As I read through my journal around the time of our move to China, some entries are not too flattering. Two

36

days in a row our family had taxi drivers that took us to the wrong place, or in the wrong direction. I lost my cool and shouted at the second driver. Angela checked my anger, asking me to show grace to people, even the incompetent. In the stress of adjusting to a new place, a new routine, I'm not demonstrating much mercy, kindness or patience.

The cross reminds us that it is precisely because we are sinners that we need the sacrifice of Christ, we need God's mercy. The cross assaults our pride, the overconfidence that thinks we can handle life on our own, we can be good enough without having to rely on God's grace totally.

About a month after arriving in China I started reading and praying through Mark, the shortest gospel. In Mark's view, Jesus is a man of action. The fast-paced plot has several moments of foreboding that point to the cross. The Passion of Jesus, his arrest, beating, crucifixion and rising again from the dead, seem to be the main point that Mark is pointing us too.

Two months after our arrival, I flew to Taiwan for a few days of training with a client. A prayer I prayed at this time: *I have two young boys, both of them new believers. How do I help them grow in their faith, especially when they spend ten hours each week day away from us at their school? When I do have time with them, I'm often impatient and not loving. I want to train them in discipline, but perhaps I'm missing what really matters—the attitude of the heart. God, I need help!*

How do we nurture faith? It has be something we are living out ourselves. We are not passing along a religion or cultural traditions. In order to pour living water into others, you cannot be moldy and stale yourself.

"Pray constantly" Paul tells us (1 Thessalonians 5:17). Read the Bible for sure, but use it to pray, to examine yourself, to direct you in how to apply truth every day in practical ways. Most of all, spend time focusing your attention on drawing in closer to Jesus. That is exactly what he told us to do.

"You pore over and study the Scriptures, thinking that in them you have eternal life. And they are really witnessing to me," Jesus said. "You don't want to come to me to have real life." John 5:38-40 (my translation)

"Abide in me, stay in me, and I will remain in you. It's just like a branch that cannot bear fruit unless attached to the main vine. None of you can bear fruit unless you abide/stay in me… If you stay in me and my words abide in you, you can ask whatever you want and it will happen." John 15:4,7

Journal - August 28, 2011 *God, you have led us as a family to China and there is little doubt that we belong here and have been brought here by you. Please prosper us here and help me to make smart decisions to grow the business and contribute to people here. Lord, bind us close together as a family. Lead us by your Spirit and show us clearly how to walk in the way of the cross.*

I look back now and I can see God certainly answered that prayer. When I pray something fervently that is rooted in God's will and seek to live it out, I will most definitely get what I am asking for.

[Chapter 11] Starved of the Cross

\Ron\   There are some things we grow up with that are so much a part of the scene that we fail to really see them. When we moved to Shanghai, the density of people living in that city really stood out to us. For me, an elevator is full if you have ten people inside. Thirty people in the same space with the overload buzzer going off was the rule in Shanghai. When I started riding the buses and metro, the rush hour crowd packed into a tight space was another example of "people density". I'm sure those who have been to India or Africa would find this nothing new, but as an outsider it did stand out to me.

The cross is a common symbol in America, so common that it has become part of the scenery. Cross on the church building—yeah, that fits. Cross on a necklace or t-shirt, we can see that pretty often. Even huge crosses worn as fashion items by pop stars aren't unusual, and it may not even carry any religious message.

The cross is not common in China. There are very few church buildings, so you don't see it in public or on buildings. It doesn't decorate or adorn the interior of homes like it does in Texas. Living in the middle of Shanghai in a rented apartment, we felt a little starved of the cross. We put up a small cross on the wall, above the flat screen TV, so we would see it often.

Like the cross he died on, Jesus is familiar to us and yet unknown. In fact, he is the most familiar stranger to many of us. My wife taught me a phrase about it in Chinese. "最熟悉的陌生人". Roughly, the most familiar stranger. In Chinese it carries a deep poignancy. We may know much about him and his teachings, but his person remains a mystery. Why did He die? Was it really necessary? His cross has to be the most familiar symbol that is strange and alien to us.

The cross was a crude frame for executions. Some people compare it to an electric chair, but I don't find the analogy very appropriate. The same culture that gave us the Coliseum where gladiators fought to the death and Christians were pitted against wild beasts also staged executions of criminals, rebels and insurgents in a public, brutal way: hung up on a cross, left to die and then left longer to expose the corpse to the vultures and the elements. The cross was more like a graphic billboard that said, "Don't mess around with the laws and might of Rome."

The laws of Rome did not allow their own citizens to be crucified. Their executions were done more "humanely." The cross was reserved for slaves, non-citizens, provincials and enemies of the state. Jesus was crucified not just as a criminal but also as one with no honorable standing in the eyes of the state, someone not even worthy of a humane execution. The cross really was a scandal and a stumbling block in the first century. We've lost that sting.

The motive behind the cross—a merciful God willing to radically demonstrate his sacrificial love—is celebrated among Christians, but I would say it too doesn't pierce us as deeply as it should. It takes a true confrontation with sin, with lostness and evil before the cross can touch us deeply and speak to our souls.

Our family experienced breakdown, a confrontation with our sin and frailty, our pettiness and superficial faith before we realized how starved of the cross we were. It certainly wasn't a pleasant experience or one we want to repeat. I'm guessing Jesus feels that same way about *his* cross. But there is a deeper wisdom in the cross that speaks to our souls and lets us experience God's truth and love in powerful ways.

What strikes me about my hunger is that I wasn't very aware of it before we went to China. When I was cruising along and getting by on something less than the cross, I didn't know how starved I was. I look back and the signs are there, but they were not dramatic or distinct enough to command my attention.

If you haven't deeply confronted the cross and felt its sting as well as its great mercy, let me suggest something. Pray for God to reveal it to you. We've written this book to share with you our story, our experience of coming to see the cross in a fresh and deeply personal way. We also hope that through these words you will develop an awareness of the cross and what it means to live life under its discipline, seeing people and even your own life purpose through new eyes.

Section 3 – Getting Back to the Cross

[Chapter 12] Acts 2 Community

"They devoted themselves to the apostles' teaching and to fellowship, to the breaking of bread and to prayer. Everyone was filled with awe at the many wonders and signs performed by the apostles. All the believers were together and had everything in common. They sold property and possessions to give to anyone who had need. Every day they continued to meet together in the temple courts. They broke bread in their homes and ate together with glad and sincere hearts, praising God and enjoying the favor of all the people. And the Lord added to their number daily those who were being saved." Acts 2:42-47.

/Angela/ "Please come," urged May, a banker's wife known to many in our Lujiazui gathering as our mentor and prayer leader.

"I don't care whether you bring any food," said May most reassuringly. "What matters to me is that you come."

And so many of us ladies did. Every Thursday clustered together in prayer support for each other, thanks to the committed stewardship of May and a few friends.

"I made some carrot cake," Janet's message beeped bright and early. "Can I bring some by?"

Then there's Mei (pronounced the same as May). "Hey, do you need uniforms?" she texted me. Before I could respond, I received another text from her. "Okay, done. Got them for you."

"I have an extra pair of bed sheets," Kat pulled me aside after a prayer meeting together. "Do you mind if I bless you with it?" When you first land in a foreign place and can't find all the designs and colors you like immediately, such gifts are a godsend.

I did not know any of these women when I first arrived in China. The only thing that threw us all together was we knew Christ and we all wanted to be like Him. Some were veterans at this expatriate game, they knew how to function and discover their place of ministry here. Others were barely hanging on as aliens themselves in this strange place, but what they learned and overcame they also shared. They passed on generously the help and resources to whoever was in need of it.

But what of people outside my fortress? My comfort zone? It seems any real follower of Christ will be asked this question by our Lord. Will I let them in? And when circumstances do not go my way, will I try to start an Acts 2 community or burrow deeper in my safe bunker?

A routine, organized and clean life centers me.

In China, there was no such luxury. Unexpected curveballs were many. I couldn't get people to stop spitting in public. Or ask grown men to not pull over their cars and pee by the roadside. It was very nice to say how we all like to live in an Acts 2 community (my secular friends say it's a global village) but really when the rubber meets the road, could we handle that much intimacy and contact? Life is messy, I am told. And it was definitely so in China. My close encounters with so many unlike me deflated any grandiose ideas that I had more grace than others. While I had many things to contribute, it was obvious to me soon enough that God had plenty more that I could learn from Him.

"We can do no great things; only small things with great love." Mother Teresa

"Ma' am, I don't think you are throwing your trash right," the social chair for my apartment complex said a few minutes after I opened the door. She explained the purpose of her visit with both tact and delicacy. Still, I was miffed, my eyebrows raised.

Two others stood next to her, looking on at me as I opened my door. A mini entourage over this? "I am a volunteer neighbor from another block," said one. The other? A nosey neighbor. Oh.

It didn't matter how nothing here made any sense to me. What mattered was, just like things made complete sense to Americans back home, things that were confusing to us foreigners made absolute sense to the local Shanghainese here. In other words, forget how I threw trash in America. In Shanghai, I had to humble myself to learn it their way.

I had a couple more calls after that visit. I became increasingly annoyed. In America, I had prided myself for having one of the cleanest trash bins on my street. My recycle bin was always full while others do not even bother to separate. How could I possibly miss the mark here especially when an awful stench greets me whenever I walk by their major refuse chute? The insult needless to say, was great. But was I designed, by a Creator we claim is good, to be small-minded?

Practice eventually made perfect. I rewired my brain for a new reminder constantly: Only edibles for pigs go into the wet trash bin. Everything else, no matter how dirty, goes into recycle. (Previously, I only recycled clean things.)

45

Soon after, I saw fewer red marks on my floor log sheet. The trash record sheet, pinned on the noticeboard for everyone to see, located next to the main lobby elevator, saw our ratings go up. No more standalone red ink but black like everybody else.

The price for willing submission lay in the greater triumph of enjoying a deeper friendship with the new neighbors. Two Springs later, Susan, the social chair, and I connected as sisterly friends. I found myself sharing tips with her as a first time mother, eager to hear what I have to say. And I? I was happy to learn one more time how community is possible anywhere with anyone if I let go of my prejudices and judging spirit.

"But God chose the foolish things of the world to shame the wise; God chose the weak things of the world to shame the strong. God chose the lowly things of this world and the despised things—and the things that are not—to nullify the things that are, so that no one may boast before him. " 1 Corinthians 1:27-30

For some 16 years, I lived in a culture where it was commonplace to tell shocking personal stories on national TV. A number of similar honest confessions took place among my non-church friends with me. Some told me how sleeping with their married bosses made it awkward for them to pass them on the corporate floors. Others try to convince me that sex mutually consented is okay.

For many years, it was hard for me to fathom that the church people I knew had ugly sides too. After all, they all looked so squeaky clean! So I ended up resenting and envying their perfect lives, robbing myself of much precious time and opportunity to be useful for God's kingdom.

In China however I rediscovered this unmistakable truth, thanks to the brave confessions of my Christian friends there, that we all have dirty stains and fall short of God's glory. (Romans 3:23)

"In my first year here," this new Christian friend told me, "I shopped. From Puxi to Pudong, you name it. If it's a fun place to go, I am there."

"And then? What happened after the first year?" I asked.

"It got boring soon after," she admitted. "Then, I found Christ."

金钱只是让人过得舒服一点吧了。 "Money only makes life a little bit more comfortable." This opinion holds much sway in this city. At the IFC mall, next to the iconic Pearl Tower, young Christian Dior girls wear white kid gloves to show you their expensive, beautifully crafted goods. Their black eyelashes flutter as they wait on customers with one singular motive: unload a lot of cash for a fleeting happiness. Like everywhere else, in our material world buying stuff, owning stuff, having stuff is fun and enjoyable. Even the non-Christian Shanghainese know the futility of chasing money. There is a phrase they like to say to make good rationalizations. 为什么要和钱过不去？ "Why argue with money?"

But in our Acts 2 community, it is like there is no time to lose. It was our second meet-up and already she was teaching me that soul-baring, helping each other grow more in Christ, is as vital as tea and food together.

"So, what brought you to China?" I asked this woman.

It is a common question many of us use to make small talk here. Typically, we all know the usual range of answers. Work. Husband. Ministry. See China. Learn Chinese.

"He had an affair here," she said matter-of-factly. I stopped eating, not sure how to proceed next. I must admit I was startled by her honesty. Convention tells me to keep quiet, change the subject but what kind of an Acts 2 believer am I if I can't even support her in this, this new friend of mine who found God in China?

"How did you find out?" I ventured to ask.

"I caught a disease." This time, she stopped eating her food and looked intently at me. "It's called V.D," came her reiteration.

"Could you get it in any other way?" I asked.

"No," she paused and deadpanned, "Only through sex." I figure no more naïve questions. This one is "forcing" me to tell my truths as she told her truths.

Generous listening is what we give each other as we spill our beans, one after another. In China, maybe it is the very transient lifestyles of many expatriates here but many of us recognized the urgency and shortness of available time together. One moment we share bed sheets, uniforms and cake. The next moment, we share without bridled inhibitions the sordid details of our lives. The heavens cannot but help split and shine its light on us at this willingness to be so vulnerable. In turn, many of us rose from spectator stands to become "fishers of men" (Matthew 4:19).

/Ron/ Look at what Jesus did with his followers. He gave them three years of learning. Even during that time he sent them out on mission trips, service projects, healing assignments; but after three years, he was gone. Then they had to really put the lessons into practice and see if these truths really work, to see if God would prove true to His promises. Jesus did not leave them alone. He gave them the freedom from sin won at the cross and also ongoing power through his Spirit to go out and make a difference. That same freedom and power is ours as well if we will let Him have us and use us.

"This is what we speak, not in words taught us by human wisdom but in words taught by the Spirit, explaining spiritual realities with Spirit-taught words. The person without the Spirit does not accept the things that come from the Spirit of God but considers them foolishness, and cannot understand them because they are discerned only through the Spirit. " 1 Corinthians 2:13-14 (my translation)

[Chapter 13] Living by Faith

"For the eyes of the Lord range throughout the earth to strengthen those whose hearts are fully committed to him."
2 Chronicles 16:9

/Angela/ "It's my 20th marriage anniversary today," I said on a breezy spring Sunday.

Huang Ayi, my weekly domestic helper, looked up at me from her cleaning and exclaimed out loud, "Mine was on Wednesday!"

I knew. I also knew she was celebrating her 20th marriage anniversary as well because I had taken note of it.

Without missing a beat, she eagerly asked, "So did 先生 (Mr.) give you anything?"

Without any need to withhold or pretend, I replied as one would to a good girlfriend, "No."

"Did yours?" I asked.

"Nothing at all," she replied.

"I guess we both have to wait for another 10 years!" I quipped. Her eyes went big at my answer and we broke into unabashed laughter instantly together.

(From my journal: November 2012)
"The truth is I am not sure I know how to pray for Ron anymore.   If I pray for all things to work out well, how does that count as prayer? After all, I am his wife. If he benefits, I too, benefit. In difficult times, I have complained to God.

That is not a prayer, is it? In times of what seemed like a becalmed sea, I lamented. I know He hears. Surely."

Real love is pressing on when you don't have the answers. It is praying when you are confused and not just giving up. Love is forgiving and laughing, certainly crying when you're hurt, and choosing to love the other not because they deserve it or it will benefit you.

I was pretty sure that this move to Shanghai would benefit Ron and our two young boys. Two years after living here, it seems it was for my benefit as well. To love another is terribly messy and sometimes even painful. God does it all the same. Love is unsentimental at heart and it gets most real when you stop trying to make it match what suits you. This new understanding, finally understood in China, set a new course of living for us and serendipitously, deeper into our Creator's heart.

Our time in Shanghai could really have been just a work-study-explore adventure time for us. But like a jealous lover, God was determined to woo us closer. The roadmap that was previously adequate fuel for the road—the Christian culture and community in the US we took for granted, uplifting worship experiences with a large crowd of like-minded believers—suddenly became insufficient for the new leg of the journey. Once everything familiar was depleted and taken away, we finally were ready to hear and depend on Him entirely. And that was when the real journey of living faith began.

"The beginning of wisdom is this: Get wisdom. Though it cost all you have, get understanding." Proverbs 4:7.

Today, we count that gift far above anything else we have ever experienced or owned.

I have attended church twenty-five years now. It feels like a long passage of time given over to this faith. Some I know have done it longer. Still, the simple truth is, it means nothing if I do not learn to step out of my boat with Jesus. China was that deeper ocean, a gift I could not appreciate at first.

I could with great effort and expense do life the US way in China. After all, Shanghai is a metropolis that rivals the likes of New York, Singapore and London. But once a journey is set onward with spiritual eyes, the tools for survival took on a different form.

I found myself praying more, reading more of the Bible and believing more in what I asked in faith. Nobody forced me to become a lover of the Word or crave so much intimacy with God. It was not automatic, but I was simply at the end of my rope and truly needed Him. I realized that if I were to get anything useful done for the Lord in China, I had better arm myself with better weapons. (Ephesians 6:10-18).

For one, my natural disposition to be bitter, whining, complaining and lamenting was not going to serve me. I could fill my prayer journal with such entries but I needed to lift my eyes to the hills and believe that "my help comes from the Lord, the Maker of heaven and earth" (Psalm 121:1-2). I had better work to reduce those entries in my journal. Instead, I asked, "Lord, talk to me and show me my way back to the Cross. Tell me once more why You sent Jesus."

And that He did. He chose the lowliest of that society and helped me see and understand where my following fell short. He put tests of every kind in my way so that I can seek His strength and later be of some use to others. There was not a sudden change or a moment

I can point to. You could say it was the full immersion experience of being away from home, in great need, and acknowledging my old ways weren't working.

Finally, I started to really use that faith muscle, those 25 years of faith experience, and take chances on the front lines. What I knew so much about in my head but took little effort to flex before finally caught up with what I was facing every day.

China, surprisingly, gave me a new lease at learning what living in faith means again. For many who are still checking out God, I must say He does have a sense of humor. Just look at the place he chose to help me know Him better. In Communist China, where there is no manifest destiny, or a special chosen lot of people, those who seek really do find. The God who parted the Red Sea, still lives and He does actually still act mightily.

And He wants us back.

[Chapter 14] Friends for the Road

How delightful to have friends visiting from afar!" - Confucius

\Ron\ We had been in Shanghai only a few months when we received our first guests. Still trying to adjust to a new place, new culture, missing our friends and loved ones back home—all of these emotions were still working on us.

In such circumstances, a visit from anyone familiar whether relative, family member, business colleague or friends would be most welcome. The saying from Confucius above is from his Analects, and it comes in the beginning of the collection, more than 2,000 years old, but the freshness of the feeling it captures rings so true.

It seems fitting that the first guests we had in Shanghai were our old friends Joe and Anna who had been at our wedding in Singapore almost 20 years before. We had not kept up close contact when we were apart, maybe once every few years. Each time we reconnected, however, seemed like a divine appointment.

Long-term friendships (and long-distance ones especially) can be captured by how easily you take up the conversation where you last left off. Is it awkward how you handle the time elapsed and the inevitable changes that have taken place? Are you stuck in either superficial topics or shared memories from the past which leave you unable to talk much about the present? Or are you able to easily catch up, to plunge deep and to appreciate the wonder of someone else's life experience as you get to re-live it in compressed time?

When Joe and Anna came to see us, we took time to eat together, to share where we were, to inquire more deeply into their own recent past, and to pray together in a deeper way.

One part of the conversation, as Angela recalls it, went like this:

"When Ron calls you on the phone, how do you know it is him?" Anna asked.

"Well, because I recognize it is his voice," I answered, surprised at her line of questioning.

"How do you know it is not someone posing to be Ron?" Anna asked again.

"Because I *just* know it is him," I said.

"And that is how we know if it is the Spirit speaking to us," she answered.

From that conversation onwards, I no longer doubt whether I hear the Spirit or not. Instead, I pray to hear Him clearly and plea for Him to help me see.

\Ron\ We talked about our own respective experiences in the local church over the past few years. We discussed the current situation in the world and what God's view of it is. This couple always seemed to have something of a prophetic insight to things, and they challenged us to bring our own views and conversations into the light of the cross.

The visit by Joe and Anna was certainly a much-needed breath of refreshing air for us and a source of ongoing reflection long after they were gone. Some parts of scripture that we often overlook came alive in fresh ways, such as Paul's own relief and refreshment when he had visitors come and share welcome news and to spend time in fellowship and prayer with him (see 1 Thessalonians 3:1-10, Philemon 17-24, Philippians 2:25-30 for examples).

Living with your back to the cross is a hard discipline. Rather than asking God to explain why things happen the way they do, we started learning to take each day on its own terms. Truthfully, the flesh does not want to accept the partial views that we are often given, the unanswered questions, the pain of missing family and friends, of being misunderstood, of feeling like you are alone. Jesus dealt with the same frustrations, sadness and disappointments. Separated from family and childhood friends, he had to walk day by day in faithfulness. He had to demonstrate faithful obedience to the Father moment by moment.

The road to the cross can get lonely, the jeers from the crowd arouse self-doubt, which is one of the primary reasons that Jesus promised to send his Holy Spirit, his Comforter and Advocate for our benefit. The way of the cross is not easy or cheerful or even certain. It is testing, trying and often full of self-doubt. But Jesus asks us to take courage in the journey, to recall we are not alone. We have him with us. We also have friends who share the faith commitment with us, who share some of the delight and also lighten the burden for us.

[Chapter 15] New Eyes to See

"What do you want me to do for you?"
"Lord, I want to see," he replied." Luke 18:41

/Angela/ In China, it appears on the surface that a lot of people are stuck in either difficult poverty or what looks like a very hard life.   Their situation looks deserving enough that it often inspires even an ordinary Christian to step up and help bring some relief to them.

Whether it is to provide a job, give some spare change or bring warmth to the soul via a simple smile or a respectful nod, I have personally witnessed many in my Christian community do that.

The people here toil long hours every day, some even seven days a week without stop. A person may have an official job but then also have side work for extra income.   They do their work quietly alongside a city bursting at its seams in growth and development. They work with loyal devotion, accepting their fates that they would never rise above the work they have chosen to do.

So the road sweeper sweeps daily without fail, on a particular street in Shanghai all seasons of the year, from sunrise to sundown.   His arms are tired and his back hurts. Still, there is no job promotion, much less a big jump in salary. The strong winds from up north blow the neatly swept leaves again.   Still, without walking away, the road sweeper picks up the mess and continues his work.   Definitely no headliner on any paper.

So goes also the man who delivers two water bottles to my apartment once a week on his three wheel bicycle.

Buzz. My apartment bell rings.

送水. "Water delivery." he calls out from the intercom.

好。请进。 "Yes. Please come in." I would dutifully respond.

Within moments, he is at my floor with those two heavy blue bottles, each bottle containing 19 liters of drinking water. How these men obtain such Herculean strength for this type of work, I have no idea.

One particular delivery guy stood out in my mind. We exchanged few details of our ives. Only a nod here, a simple hello and a thank you. Yet this 50ish gentleman, looking so much like a Chinese version of a Colin Powell, arrested my attention from the get go.

His clothes were the distinguishable sky blue uniform but he carried a spirit about him. Like many of the old guards in China, their lives read difficult. But for a great number of these folks, they sought neither personal vanity nor pride to bail them out of their hardship or place in life. The Chinese have a phrase for it, this spirit of acceptance of one's place in life. We call it "认命" (ren min).

In America, we think it a strange concept and label it fatalism, wanting to dismiss it. Entire industries are built on self-improvement and bettering one's life. Yet there is something deeply admirab e about being "认命", accepting one's place under the heavens, accepting the cross we each are given to bear. One is not resigned or annoyed at all. One simply works with full acceptance and whole heart on the task accorded to them. It is not much different from a mature follower of Christ. We love when we cannot. We forgive when patience runs thin. We press on even when it is hard.

The Christian faith certainly has its difficult mountains to bear. Take this passage on love for instance, an exhortation of what love is from the apostle Paul.

Love is patient, love is kind. It does not envy, it does not boast, it is not proud. It does not dishonor others, it is not self-seeking, it is not easily angered, it keeps no record of wrongs. Love does not delight in evil but rejoices with the truth. It always protects, always trusts, always hopes, always perseveres.   *1 Corinthians 13:4-7*

It is hard practice. So many of us prefer to abandon living all these truths out sometimes. But God does not allow me to cherry pick.

I think about the baker spinning out hot tortillas every day. Or the school bus driver promptly arriving each day at the same spot to pick up kids. I think of the preacher who never fails to prepare and lead the congregation into worship, no matter the size, or the mom who cooks daily, scanning and exchanging recipes online to create good family meals. Working in silence, without accolades and still doing our jobs well.

In Shanghai, many folks are like the water delivery guy. They go about their work with no time to think or ask that it be full of meaning. Neither do they request for it to be pleasurable. Certainly they do not expect the work they do to make them rich.

Still, with dignity and complete uncomplaining, they work. Their faces exude natural grace and serenity.

Lovers of God, Christians who follow the Cross are not very different from these ordinary folks in China. They too, I believe, have found something paranormal, something where the surface tells only half the story. God, awake us from our slumber. Help us see life and people in a new way.

[Chapter 16] New Attitude at the Office

"Whatever you do, work at it with all your heart, as working for the Lord, not for men since you know you will receive an inheritance from the Lord as a reward. It is the Lord Christ you are serving." Colossians 3:23-24

\Ron\ I enjoy working alone. In fact, in almost every job I've had there was a great amount of freedom to do the work as I saw fit. When I went to China it was not really that different. The formal working relationship was loosely defined. The main difference is that for the first time I was working often in a traditional office arrangement. This was new for me.

I had worked in an industrial shop with heavy equipment, in a retail store, in a church, in a university and for over a decade from home as a business consultant who traveled on site to my clients. I had been fairly effective at keeping up high walls between my faith and my working identity. At work, I tried to be professional, which meant people didn't know much about my beliefs, and I could maintain my privacy.

Shanghai is a working city, the most developed commercial center in China. To call it the New York City of China is probably a fair analogy. Increasingly, multinationals are locating their Asia-Pacific headquarters there to secure their place in the China market and the larger region. In the skyscraper downtown area of Pudong called Lujiazui lies the financial center with soaring bank towers and the Shanghai Stock Exchange. This is where our office was, on the 17th floor of a tall office building.

This city has a youthful energy to it. The working force tilts toward the young and they have a hunger to learn, to get ahead, to prosper and be recognized for their efforts. In the office what people lack in experience they are willing to compensate for with hustle and effort. Working at close quarters with colleagues and especially a junior staff was a new experience for me.

Company cultures are something I work with and help leaders to understand and to shape. I have learned that there is a great variety within different worksites. One of the key differences is the kind of conversations that take place inside. Do people exchange small talk or social chat? Do they care about each other as people and not just as fellow workers? Is the culture hard on newcomers or welcoming? Are roles well-understood or vague? Is the work well organized or chaotic? These and other factors are all part of the company culture.

Culture expresses the core conversations we keep having. The richness or emptiness of a culture is found in the quality (or poorness) of the conversations. Culture does not maintain a vacuum. Something will always fill it. The question is, are you contributing to or influencing what that is?

To take part in an organization and to be a player in the culture is very different from observing and studying it as someone on the outside. Most people are participants and don't have the chance to be consultants, which is like the difference between a fish in the ocean and a marine biologist on land. Another way to see it is being a student at school versus being a parent of a school-going child. Those are two very different experiences. Each has their unique vantage points, but the quality of the experience is completely different.

What happened as I got involved in the small firm in Shanghai and took part in conversations with partners, colleagues, and junior staff on both a professional and personal level was an unveiling. Besides learning about other people, their life stories and individuality, perhaps the biggest surprise is what I learned about myself.

I had seen myself before as an intelligent, responsible professional. Working alone or in small teams with other colleagues at client sites allowed me to develop professional skills that were in demand in the workplace as a management consultant. Now in another culture, in a fast-moving city and competitive market I saw new parts of myself that before had been either hidden from me or unchallenged.

I had years of experience, but not all of it was relevant to a less mature developing market. Translating it into another language also presented challenges. Showing understanding and providing guidance to others deepened my empathy even while I let go of my overconfidence and pride.

The reality of office politics came alive in new ways. You don't eliminate politics, but you do get to choose where to engage and where you don't. Not every battle is worth fighting; wisdom lies in knowing which ones matter.

In this environment, I faced new faith challenges as well. Around me there seemed to be a spiritual vacuum. When the main focus is on material pursuits, the hunger and thirst of the soul grows. "Isn't there something more?" it cries.

How would I speak as a witness into this void? I found Paul's counsel in the first century an especially appropriate piece of wisdom. "Do your work, whatever it is, with all your heart, as working for the Lord, not for men. Know that you will receive an inheritance from the Lord as a reward in this. The truth is, it is the Lord Christ you are serving." Colossians 3:23-24

Yes, there is more than money and titles and climbing the ladder and buying bigger and better things. There is a call to come and die, to follow Christ to the cross and to lay down your illusions and false dreams to embrace a bigger vision of His kingdom.

I found young working professionals who organized lunchtime sessions near high-tech industrial parts and in financial centers, in teaching hospitals and other places in which they shared management lessons and wisdom as well as their own life story. Young colleagues eager to learn turned out for these sessions to see what it was all about. What could they learn? Curiosity often led to more earnest seeking for answers to questions as spiritual life was nurtured and grew.

Besides these workplace lunch sessions, there were nighttime home meetings where we would gather for dinner together followed by some sharing and study from the Bible and prayer together. These meetings attracted working professionals, both believers and those with little knowledge or background in spiritual matters. The gospel stories of Jesus provided us a focal point.

My own discomfort and inadequacies for this work didn't really matter. If I allowed them to stop me as I had many times before, it would simply leave the vacuum open for other voices to rise up and other answers to be offered. The soul cannot tolerate a vacuum for long. The call for me was to come back to the cross. Be willing to serve. Be willing to die and face the difficulties or embarrassment. In the cross is hope, healing and deep truth.

The empty antics and routines of the office can be redeemed. It takes servants willing to carry the message there in jars of clay, far from perfect messengers who are ready to let the Spirit work in surprising ways to call them and others back to the cross.

[Chapter 17] A New Look at Work

\Ron\   I live in a very privileged place in China. Lujiazui is the financial epicenter of Shanghai, somewhat like Wall Street or the City (of London), an aspiring financial center for Asia. The Stock Exchange is just down the street, an easy walk on my way to the office. Out my kitchen window I can see three iconic Pudong buildings: the Jinmao Tower, the Shanghai World Financial Center (current tallest building in China, rising up 100 floors) and the Shanghai Center (will be the tallest building in China when completed).

There are plenty of wealthy bankers, business people and office workers in this area by day. You also see five story walkup apartments for local residents known commonly as *laobaixing* (the common people). In the alleys and side streets of these local apartment buildings you can find the goods and services that are more affordable for those on a budget: the Wenzhou barbershop where my boys and I get a haircut for US$2, the clean and simple restaurant run by a retired Taiwanese man we call Frank, serving home style Chinese food, the fruit seller over by the dirty market where few expatriates shop, and the egg seller who always greets me warmly and sells the best eggs for frying. These are the hard working people that I support who are not on the expensive street fronts, driving hard bargains for marked-up goods to those who have more disposable incomes.

As I walk by I think: *I know your hard work, that you labor day in and day out to make ends meet. You won't get rich, but if you stay at it you will make a living. You are not scholars or learned people; what you know is hard work. But what you teach me is a valuable lesson about staying at your post, showing up for work and getting the job done. It is a hard day's work, but you do it without loud complaints or protest.*

"Where do people get this work ethic?" I wonder to myself. It is a necessary thing in order to build a society. However, fewer people are willing to do it. In the US it seems fewer people are willing to do the manual jobs of working on construction sites and cleaning houses, bringing in the harvest or picking up the garbage. These jobs go to those willing to work these jobs, which is more often migrant labor or sometimes the new immigrants. Here in Shanghai it is a similar situation. Those who are true locals, who are from Shanghai and grew up here don't wish to take these manual jobs; they usually go to those from distant provinces who have come to the city to work, migrant workers who find more opportunity here than back home.

As I reflect on these workers, my thoughts also go to my parents who came from working families who lived in small towns of the Central and Southwest United States. They came from a background that demanded hard work in order to get ahead. Both of my parents showed an example of being unafraid of hard work, a willingness to roll the sleeves up and get it done.

When Jesus came into this world, he was not born into privilege or comfort. His parents did not live in the thin middle or elite upper parts of Jewish society in Galilee. He was the son of a carpenter, a tradesman.

Nazareth was not far from Sepphoris, a prosperous Hellenized city that probably provided steady work for Joseph. Jesus would have frequently visited the city, probably learned to speak the common Greek tongue shared by the Romans, Jews and foreigners living there, and he learned to work hard from his father's example and due to simple necessity. His family lived in the village and was familiar with the agricultural cycle and rhythms of life of their neighbors.

Jesus' stories that he used for teaching spoke of sowing seed and harvesting crops, of women with lost coins and fathers with dutiful sons as well as rebellious ones who squandered the family fortune on "fast living" in far-off lands. He was very familiar with traditional Jewish wedding feasts and pilgrimage to Jerusalem to worship at the temple. He also knew who was in power and how politics worked, whether it was the religious establishment ruled by the priests or real rulers who were Romans and their client kings such as the Herodian family.

When Jesus called an inner circle of followers to live closely with him and learn from him, he called the sons of fishermen, tradesmen and tax collectors, insurgents who were recently made landless--called Zealots—in other words, he felt at home with and invested his life in the common people, the hard workers rather than the rich young men or the educated or the religious who came from the leading families.

These were people who would not have instinctively balked at hardship and suffering. The call to follow him, to live on the run and one step ahead of the powerful who felt threatened by Jesus and who plotted his death, this was something they could accept.

What they found harder to accept was the demonstration of unconditional love, the call to forgive their enemies, the grace and mercy that Jesus revealed as being the very essence and heart of his Father. And of course these hard-working, proud people could not accept laying down your life and dying shamefully on a cross and surrendering without putting up a good fight. This was unthinkable.

When it all happened this way, there was shock and denial and disillusionment, confusion. Had it all been vain, a very cruel joke? It was inconceivable when one of the women returned fushed and breathless saying, "He has risen! He is no longer in the tomb but has been raised!" These were simple men, but not stupid. This sounded like nonsense...yet Peter and John scrambled to get out the door and raced to the tomb. They confirmed the unbelievable for themselves. It was as Mary the Magdalene had said, and before too long they were to see with their own eyes, and still later even Thomas would feel with h s own fingers the scars and healed wounds and come lately to his own belief.

The call to take up the cross and to carry the good news to the nations was laid upon these men and women. The real hard work was just beginning.

It continues today. The hard work of believing even in the face of contrary circumstances, of laboring to bring good news to distant lands, to mountain tribes, to the cities and to displaced peoples, the hard work of raising and educating the young, of healing the sick and feeding the hungry, of giving hope to the hopeless and preaching to the imprisoned, this is what it really means to come back to the cross, to put our backs to the cross and submit to its stern discipline and to find in the cross the true hope of the world.

"But we preach Christ crucified, a stumbling block to Jews and foolishness to Gentiles, but to those whom God has called, both Jews and Greeks, Christ the power of God and the wisdom of God. For the foolishness of God is wiser than man's wisdom, and the weakness of God is stronger than man's strength." 1 Corinthians 1:23-25

69

[Chapter 18] Welcoming Help at Home: Huang Ayi

The first time I met 小黄 ("Xiao Huang"), I was struck by the effects of toil on what appeared to be a fairly young woman. Her spirit seemed heavy from continuous work.

It was on a Sunday when we met. There was a ring at my apartment doorbell around 10 am.

你是谁？ "Who is it?" I asked over the intercom.

我听说也许你有工作。 "I was told that you might have a job for me," came a soft female voice from downstairs.

I then vaguely recalled that I had mentioned to Shi Ayi a need for some cleaning help.

Do I ask her to come up now or do I turn her down? After all, I could easily turn her away since I was only a few weeks into this new country. I was still adjusting, and though having cleaning help was a welcome, I did not have enough mental space to consider an outside person in our house. But maybe I was overthinking this and making it a bigger deal than it was. What better way to test the waters than by just jumping in?

So I did. I let her into our home. Into my very private life.

That trial period of four hours soon turned to be a weekly job. Things were not always done right. I had to learn whether it was about me or it was God's way of putting us together to learn something from one another.

I still remember vividly the scene to consider the ethereal significance behind this connection. I was reading my Bible, journal at hand. She was ironing our clothes at the dining table next to me.

"Here," she said, eyes still on the shirt she was ironing but her head motioned to a card she had placed on the table.

"I thought you might want some details about me," she continued. It was her Chinese government issued ID card.

For Xiao Huang, placing her ID card before me with her head bowed while still ironing our clothes made me pause.

"Here, take." Her quiet action spoke in a loud volume. Trust me...please. The unspoken was said so elegantly that my heart had to pause to soak it all in.

So, I did. Her desire to work, to earn extra income for her family was an inspiring act in itself.

太太，不好意思。我的电车坏了。正拿去修理。会耽误一些。再过十五分就到。"Madam, I am so sorry. My electric scooter just broke down. It is being repaired now so I will be 15 minutes late."

I have a low tolerance for tardiness but what Xiao Huang taught me was, sometimes being late was not a slight. Things happen, and I need to learn to go with the flow. Her son forgets the house key and she had to turn around on her way over to settle the mess. It is winter and raining cats and dogs. Still, she comes in the rain on her electric scooter. Through Huang Ayi, I saw how the majority of the less educated Chinese work in the city. Their hours are long but their work ethic is admirable.

How do you support and nurture a willing servant? You teach her more. You look for ways to help her win. "I do not know how to cook," she tells me. "Ok, cut onions and garlic then," I say, "Make enough for a week." And so this is how Xiao Huang got to spend more time at our small apartment.

Like any other human being, I have noise and personal distractions of my own to entertain myself rather than notice someone else's needs first. With her weekly predictable time at our apartment, God seemed to say, "Look. Notice. Look again." God gave me a new set of eyes for seeing service help in my home.

It became clear very quickly that having Huang Ayi in my life was more than just help around the house or extra income for her. The time together, spent in the intimate setting of a home, gave us both a peek into another world we normally would not step into.

Through her, I was able to see the clothes millions of ordinary scooter riders had to wear to bear the freezing cold and rain as they move about the city without the warmth of a car. With such an inspiring example, it was only natural for a Jesus follower like me to up my game as well. I learned to let go of petty upsets and unrealistic expectations. In other words, to not be so small-minded.

Could I be like Huang Ayi and the many like her in the way I conduct my business in life? To work in silence. To work in subservience. To bow down even further. To not retaliate but treat my boys in kindness even when they were not deserving of it? To generously listen to my widowed mother, be her listening friend, even when my "scooter" breaks down and is depleted for that day?

Over time, I learned to also let go of my fears and entrusted her with keys to our apartment when we were out of town. She cleaned and did what was needed and then would quietly leave, like an elf who transformed our place of laundry and dishes piled high and restored it to one with love and welcome order.

Gradually, I grew to care for this stranger in my house. This stranger, whom I knew so little about in the beginning and found myself developing a deep caring and responsibility for. Through her humble attitude and faithful work, she taught me what true humility was about. Though our possessions were few in China, I desired to erect a wall around me as well. But by giving me Huang Ayi, God taught me there is greater joy when you include "strangers" along in your life.

So I stepped out of my neuroses, hushed the justification for distance between me and others and let His Spirit be poured once more into me.

"When did we see a stranger and invite you in, or needing clothes and clothe you?"
"I tell you the truth, whatever you did for one of the least of these brothers of mine, you did for me." (Matthew 25:38, 40)

[Chapter 19] A New Look at Healthcare

/Angela/ I am pushed from all sides. People behind me nudge me forward. The mass of bodies come at me like tsunami waves. I don't like it one bit. But, this is China, the real China.

I am standing in the reception area of 东方医院 (Shanghai East Hospital) in Lujiazui, which is one of the better public hospitals in China. I'm not upstairs in the international division where the crowds are fewer and the prices are higher. I am among the Chinese where it costs less than US$2 (10 RMB) to see a doctor.

The system, the process or where to go—it all confounds me. It just looks and sounds chaotic to me. I'm not in the ER; I have decided my blood pressure and the throbbing in the back of my head finally needs some attention. The Chinese doctor who practices traditional Chinese medicine said he can't bring it down. He tells me I need western medicine.

I don't have international health insurance. The budget just wouldn't allow it, and we don't have a big company sponsoring us here. The previous private clinic I visited here, the one that caters to expatriates, charged almost US$100 for the consultation. I remember the Singaporean doctor there urging me to buy some international health insurance when I shared our situation with him.

I really do not like spending time in the medical system. I've spent more time than I care to in hospitals and doctor's clinics in Singapore, the US, and China. I am grateful when medical science can help us with our problems. I have also seen firsthand its limitations and shortcomings.

One can get medical help most anywhere in this world. There is a reason that people are willing to travel, even internationally, to Mexico or India or the US, for medical care. You can spend a little or a lot, and what you pay doesn't always guarantee a better outcome.

The real question I have had to face is this: when you are sick, how are you going to handle it? If you have any financial means, the typical answer is to go see a doctor. Why isn't our first impulse to pray and seek healing from God? I suspect that we don't believe healing is really in His hands.

I battle the unbelief in myself. I have received prayers and healing and thanked God for it. I have also prayed and not seen any change in my body or symptoms for months.

Perhaps this is why our Savior came. God knows our life here is temporal. What does matter is eternity with Him.

When I let Him in, I am cleansed. I am cleaned up, like the way a hot shower does me good after a day of grime, smoke and smog, of being out and about in the city. Only better. My soul gets healed. I receive nothing less than a greater capacity for love. It is only because He lives in me that I am changed.

No matter where we are, we may sometimes find ourselves a cure for our physical ailment. Or maybe not. The quest to full healing I suspect does not end in full physical healing alone.

God wants to give us the "peace of Christ" that "transcends all understanding". (Philippians 4:7).

Will I just stop and rest? Could I simply tell Him how sad I am feeling? Will I give up trying so hard to be in control? Or finally tell Him that I am just afraid and could use some help?

How about simply letting the hurt and disappointment or anger go? Because I can be old, grey-haired, frail bones, sitting in a wheelchair, rich or poor, but still, true real health of the soul eludes me.

Will I give Him that gift?

I need to find out how He can heal me and relentlessly pursue that answer instead of all sorts of things that do not get me very far.

Let Him take care of all my hurts, disappointments and fears? Yes.

If I start with these, I might even start to see who Christ really is and why He came. I can pursue that understanding. It is a gift I can give my God and no one can take that away from me.

The hospital is chaotic, though I am learning the system. But the ways of Grace, I am still just beginning to learn to live in them.

[Chapter 20] A New Look at Real Wealth

"Of what value is an idol carved by a craftsman?
Or an image that teaches lies?
For the one who makes it trusts in his own creation;
he makes idols that cannot speak.
Woe to him who says to wood, 'Come to life!'
Or to lifeless stone, 'Wake up!'
Can it give guidance?
It is covered with gold and silver;
there is no breath in it."
The Lord is in his holy temple;
let all the earth be silent before him." Habakkuk 2:18-20.

/Angela/ Make no mistake about it. There are many people who have found the formula to make piles of money in Shanghai. I think that explains why luxury brands like Burberry, Louis Vuitton and Prada go crazy in their store expansion efforts in this country.

Yet, with all this wealth around, it wasn't the rich whose comfortable lives gave me the most support and inspiration to live my days in China. Rather, it was the scores of men and women in the city who worked the underbelly jobs here: the maintenance guy from Anhui, the driver who experienced bitter humiliation during the Cultural Revolution, the noodle-selling Muslim family from Xinjiang and the well-tanned faces of men and women who sold me vegetables and fruit daily by the "dirty" market. I also cannot forget the simple old man whose sole sale each day by the corner of a fruit stall are his signature huge fresh clams he dug up himself.

For millions of such individuals in this country, there is no real holiday or break. It only makes sense that train stations are stuffed to the gills during the Chinese New Year. Viewers at home may shake their heads at this incredible mass exodus of human migration within this country. But wouldn't you want to go home if all you do year-round is mundane work like a ticking clock and hardly a break?

我早上六点就到。先生半夜十二点就到市场. Basically, my veggie seller is sharing details of her daily routine with me when I found her sorting the vegetables at 7:30 one early morning. She tells me that "she is there from 6 in the morning. Her husband goes to the wholesale market at midnight."

It is one thing to be told to persevere in faith like James 1:2-4 says. It is another to watch someone in action who is persevering. Their work ethic and spirit to serve their customers brings me a new understanding of the verse like nothing before.

I have watched them fight. I have heard their complaints, her upsets, his embarrassment. Then comes her acknowledgment that maybe she was impulsive too, followed by his acknowledgment that maybe she does have a point.

Still, they worked. They made sure each day their inventory of vegetables is collected, then packaged neatly in small bundles for customers to survey and buy. He takes his afternoon naps and then does his deliveries while she constantly rearranges her supply of vegetables on display like a mom fusses over a young toddler.

To be sure, many people in different places work long hours. In Singapore where I grew up, long hours are common too. But what is it about this side of Shanghai that won my heart? I believe it is the people's spirit.

They smile genuinely even when life is hard. After all, who doesn't have long and difficult days? They endure without ever receiving kudos from anyone. I have learned a lot about what it is to work, "to give my best", "as one approved by God" from them. (2 Timothy 2:15)

Real wealth is not earned or understood through might or power. "By my Spirit," says the Lord Almighty in Zechariah 4:6.

I have to wonder, "Who is really wealthy?" The ones with money but empty eyes, stalked by depression, or the ones who work hard with spirit and with perseverance, who have few pretensions?

[Chapter 21] A New Look at Consumption

/Angela/ My husband often leads me to places I am not comfortable going. One of those places was a bustling but unremarkable alley near our apartment where you could buy fresh eggs of all types for a song. I resisted going there for months. Finally I gave up resisting God and went. The egg lady was finally glad to meet me after months of seeing my husband and boys.

"So, you are the mom!" she said happily. Her friendliness immediately thawed my guardedness. After a few transactions together, I finally found courage to ask her what she did with her cracked or broken eggs.

"We eat them," she said and broke into an embarrassed smile. Our eyes met in a tender moment.

"Do you not eat the good ones?" I asked, feeling half awkward at my intrusion.

"Oh no, those are for the customers," she responded in gracious acceptance.

I used to think certain parts of the Bible are only decodable and its meaning unlocked by a few very smart and lucky Bible scholars. So as a regular church goer, I really did not have to work hard at seeing or learning.

In China, I began to change my mind about that. After our shared "secret" that day, it was no longer just me popping in to buy eggs from my egg lady but a chance to observe quiet service, patience and much forbearing at work. Here in this uninspiring, undistinguished alley, my egg lady in her gentle unassuming way helped open my spiritual eyes. It is a gift I am most thankful for. She demonstrated by her life's example what Matthew 5:6 truly meant.

"Blessed are the meek, for they will inherit the earth"
(Matthew 5:6)

[Chapter 22] Eat Soy Sauce

"Create in me a pure heart, O God, and renew a steadfast spirit within me."
Psalm 51: 10

/Angela/ Just before our missions trip to Anhui, I mentioned to my husband my immense difficulty in fasting. I loved to eat, and for me to go without food for no obvious or pressing need seemed an incredibly hard thing to do.

"Well, you can go without meat," he suggested.

I winced. "Too hard," I replied.

"What about eating rice with just soy sauce?" he offered, trying *hard* to be helpful. It was a great idea. Still, it was unappetizing and had no appeal to it.

"I might as well not eat," I challenged.

"It's like, what's the point of eating then, right?" he teased.

"Yes," I smiled sheepishly. But I did so today.

When I said "yes" to our church mission trip to the inland (and less developed) province of Anhui, I suspected that it was the beginning of something new. I felt I needed to prepare myself ahead so that it didn't turn into just a nice adventure holiday with a bunch of Christians.

So I ate soy sauce and plain rice.

I stripped myself of things I normally would eat and fasted on the simplest foods that day.

The insight soon came, as they always do in stillness and seeking.

As I ate rice with plain soy sauce, I saw a vision of what it must have been like for the many poor people in China. I have seen some of them around in Shanghai. "Their meals are so simple," I think to myself. When first seen through sated eyes I am so dense I ask myself the question, "Why do they bother to eat?"

"Because that is all they can afford," I answered my sons when I finally saw the answer. They too had the same question as I.

I gave thanks. As I ate each bite, I gave thanks. For the things that brought me here thus far and for the things to come. For the people I knew and met and for the people I would meet and know soon.

I normally am a fast eater but the deliberate slow down had a humbling effect on me. As I chewed a bite of rice with soy sauce in my mouth, my thanks came from the deepest part of me, a side of me I usually do not visit because life is full of things to do.

I gave thanks for the people I would meet again and for the good we would do as a Body of Christ. And for the lessons we would draw for ourselves. Would I discipline myself and choose to see good? Or would I be repulsed by some habits that have gagged me here in Shanghai and had me live in a siege mentality as an expat for months? The mission trip was still weeks away, yet already, I was asked to examine myself. Maybe the trip had already begun and I was just now realizing it.

Section 4 – Come Follow Me

[Chapter 23] What's Needed?

/Angela/ Over twenty years ago, a kindly professor named John Willis shared Micah 6:8 when he was teaching a church group in Singapore. I was young as a Christian and the verse filled me up like fresh water for a thirsty soul.

"... And what does the Lord require of you? To act justly and to love mercy and to walk humbly with your God." Micah 6:8.

\Ron\ Even though Angela and I were together at that church, I could not recall this lesson or event as vividly as she could. I am grateful for her memory, for it brought back to me an earlier episode from my life before we even met.

In the spring of 1987 I had my first Bible class with a real Bible professor. The class was taught by John Willis and the subject was Job-Malachi. Willis was an expert on the Old Testament, but what impressed me even more was that he made the effort to remember the names of the 200 students in this class! I also remember that he gave out cookies in every class, and he invited his students over to his home during the semester.

John did his doctoral work at Vanderbilt University in the 1960's, and it so happened that he did his thesis on Micah. As a young man of 19, I still remember that he taught me Micah 6:6-8 and in a matter-of-fact way commented that people persistently try to "substitute an hour of worship [on Sunday] for a week of righteous living." John modeled for me what it looked like to act justly, love mercy, and to walk humbly with God.

The only other person I've known personally who kept all three of these in balance was Angela. In Shanghai she was frequently led to help the poor, or to serve individuals or the church in some quiet way that often involved our whole family. Only she knows how often she has had to put up with my pride and try to point me to the way of the cross, which teaches us true humility.

We have been confronted by the cross and challenged to change how we think, to soften our hearts, our attitudes. In this section, we will look at what it looks like to answer Jesus' call to "come follow me." While in Shanghai we were continually led to face each of these realities: *act justly, love mercy, walk humbly with God*. We will use Micah 6:8 as a three-dimensional description of what is needed for the life of following Jesus.

[Chapter 24] Woman at the Well

/Angela/ I can only offer her water. Deep down, the demon of "it's-not-your-business" fights to win. I so badly wish to be like my Savior, Jesus. To comfort, to stand up for the weak, to speak against unrighteousness with grace. I want to walk on but something in me, when in China, makes me stop. So, I start with a cup of water. Here, please take. A drink for you.

I have watched this woman's faithfulness for several seasons now. Come rain or shine, bone-chilling cold or sunny skies, this woman sweeps the sidewalks and keeps the street in front of our complex free of trash. I have watched her sweep a pile of dead leaves, only to have it be scattered behind her again by a gust of strong wind. Still, she sweeps. China is like that, full of faithful hands, quiet and obedient to their tasks. Today was no different. She sweeps but something awful must have happened.

As I returned from a delightful meeting with co-workers, I was greeted by a raucous commotion on my street. It seems a crowd always gathers when something out of the ordinary happens.

Upon looking closer, I realized a fellow street sweeper—probably her senior or the foreman—was berating the woman who swept in front of my complex. Whatever it was, the woman was upset – crying and ranting. The beasts inside her had been set loose by the attack she had just suffered.

In the city often the best way to survive is to shut out all noise and ignore everything. Walk on by. But something inside was not allowing me to do that. I stopped to observe the commotion, now attracting more attention. I then caught sight of a sister in Christ on the sidewalk. Her appearance gave me courage. Can we extend grace like our Savior?

"Wait here for me," I told her. "I am going to get a cup of water for her. Stay here, I need courage," I say.

I understood hardly a word of Shanghainese. But I know when a person feels aggrieved and when a person feels that no one is listening. So I let her give vent to her grievances and hurts. After a while I said in Mandarin, the lingua franca understood commonly here, "Stop. Please stop. Whatever it is, let it go."

"I have watched you. I know you are doing your job." The words came with both confidence and an authority I know was not my own. Suddenly she stopped her sobbing and looked up. She smiled as she let grace be heard in her heart amid the din of noise that so often captures our heads.

She finally accepted my bottle of water.

Jesus once met a woman at a well. He could have silently let her draw her water and then go home, but he chose to engage her in conversation and offer her water. This street sweeper was like my woman at the well. All I did was stop and talk with her, offer a bottle of water. In that simple act, I let Jesus speak a deeper truth to her. I love how China is changing my heart.

[Chapter 25] Hiddenness

"I...present to you God's word in its fullness, the mystery kept hidden for ages and generations but is now revealed to the believers." Colossians 1:26

\Ron\ Here is something to ponder. If we didn't have the New Testament, there would be no written record of what happened on a hill called Golgotha outside of Jerusalem in the first century. Think about that. Jesus of Nazareth dying on the cross was a non-news item in his day outside of his community of believers.

Well, not exactly. Look at Luke 24:17-24 as two of Jesus' followers fully expected someone they saw as a recent visitor to Jerusalem to know the fresh news about what had happened to Jesus. He was widely known among the Jews as a powerful prophet, recently crucified, reputed to be raised to life again.

Paul in writing to the Christians in Rome, a city he had not visited and a church he did not personally establish, could refer to a common knowledge about Jesus, his death and resurrection (Rom 1:4, 3:22-26, 5:6-10, 8:32-34).

The first century world was an oral society and news usually traveled by word of mouth. The majority of people did not read, there were no newspapers or other media that we take for granted. The main writings were official documents of the government and literary writings for the educated elites. The account of Jesus' death and the subsequent growth of the church apparently gained no notice in official and literary circles.

There was a hidden quality to the gospel message because it was new and not widely known. We treasure the latest and newest in the modern world, but in the ancient world, tradition and stories of old were highly regarded and trusted. The earliest Christians pointed to the Jewish prophets and scriptures as a time-honored source that foretold Jesus' coming.

In China and in fact much of Asia, the gospel still has this hidden quality. Coming from the West where we take for granted that people know some basic facts about Jesus, the Bible, the cross, it is striking that the story of Jesus is little-known and intriguing. The message of the cross is fresh and arresting. People who believe in Christ are not very visible, nor are church buildings or Christian leaders. Outside of countries like the Philippines, and increasingly in South Korea and Singapore, the gospel remains hidden.

Some of the most significant things happen in hiddenness. Jesus used the example of a seed that must first fall to the ground and die before life begins and grows, first in hiddenness (John 12:24). He also taught about the miraculous process of seed growing from something tiny and hidden to something substantial (Mark 4:26-32).

I came to have a special appreciation for some of Paul's co-workers who are mentioned in passing in the New Testament. People have heard of Timothy, Titus, Barnabas, and perhaps Silas because of their mention in Acts or because they had letters addressed in their name.

It is easy to miss others like Epaphras (important in the Colossian church as well as Nympha and Archippus), Tychicus (Ephesians), Epaphroditus

(Philippians), Stephanas, Fortunatus and Achaicus along with Priscilla and Aquila in Corinth, Phoebe in Cenchrea, and a host of over 20 people named in Rome. In fact, there are even more names than I have listed here, around 50 in all that are associated with Paul's life. Of course there are even more unnamed people that were important Christ followers in the first century world, but they didn't write anything or cross the path of a letter writer like Paul or make the final cut in Luke's two volume gospel and story of the early church.

After the first century and into the second and third and every century since there have been unnamed heroes and heroines of faith who have risked much and suffered greatly and labored tirelessly so that the gospel could come down to you and me.

I was invited to step into this river of hidden disciples while in China where beyond the visible church many millions meet in house churches and minister outside the official registry.

I also got a different challenge to step out of my comfort zone of teaching adults and working with leaders in the business world. I saw myself as equipped to speak to adults using grown-up vocabulary and nuanced concepts. In China for some reason I repeatedly was called on to teach children.

At first I thought it was a mistake. Me? Teaching children? No way! My mind (and ego, if I'm honest) resisted it. I'm not called to teach children! But that is where the need is... And I recalled a conversation in the US with a sister who served full time over a children's ministry about the receptivity and cruciality of reaching this generation before they grow up and become " inoculated" to the gospel. It pierced my heart to consider the need and opportunity we have. So I went back to basics and had to learn again how to teach another group of people—little people—in hiddenness.

I found Jesus there. And the cross. Because the way of the cross is about sacrificing the ego and what makes earthly sense so that God's Spirit can teach us something real, something truly wonderful and unexpected, something that in the most improbable way is really good news. That is the essence of the cross.

"I am waging war for you...that you may really know the mystery of God, which is Christ, in whom are hidden all the treasures of wisdom and knowledge." Colossians 2:2b-3

[Chapter 26] My Shanghai Knockout Girls

/Angela/ In Shanghai, a load of knockout girls is easy to find. Right there, on Huai Hai Road, minutes from my Lujiazui apartment and across the Renmin tunnel, stunning beauties appear in the most fashionable clothes that even other women stop to look. And it's not just in one neighborhood. Women all over Shanghai dress fashionably, making almost every street a sort of runway. Many men, whether they are rich, powerful or dirt poor, cannot resist them. So the rumor is true that if you want to stray here in Shanghai you certainly can.

Another set of beauties are in this cosmopolitan place that may escape your eye. In my Shanghai, the knockout girls are the ones who tend to their stalls and shops while their husbands nap in the afternoons or make delivery runs. They dutifully sit in their stands or storefronts and wait on customers in bone-penetrating cold or stuffy sticky heat. There is sometimes weariness in their soul and a complaining word may leave their mouths but their actions betray a devotion and loyalty to the "I-do's" they promised their spouse.

They wake up daily before the sun is up and lay in their stalls the fresh eggs, veggies, fruits, meats and fish that their husbands collected fresh from the wholesale markets after midnight. There is little opportunity for chit chat or fanciful dreams for the future. Night and day, they labor. Days roll into weeks, weeks into months and months become years. Once in a while, fierce fights break out and I have witnessed a few. But the partnership they commit themselves to under such back-breaking and mundane work is unlike any love I have seen.

Typically in many married situations I know of, most women enjoy a break. The husband brings in the bacon and the woman keeps the house. Or in other marriages where both the husband and wife work, there is a housekeeper or maid service to put things around the house in order.

The women I'm speaking of do not have such luxuries. They work tirelessly in their stalls, and when night falls, they go home and do their part. One learns very quickly what it is to sacrifice for the greater good and how to live a quiet life, minding your own business and working with your hands. (1 Thessalonians 4:11)

These women don't return to fancy homes. They don't have beautiful diamonds or fun getaways to brighten up their Christmas. They stay in cramped and poorly lit apartment homes. Some wear gaiters to protect their arms. They all wear extra thick layers of clothing in the blistering cold winter and look like puffed up dolls. They are eager to sell you their goods with one eye on you, ready to serve and never missing a beat to greet another new customer. "Come," they say, "Buy from me. My fish/veggies are fresh today!"

嫁鸡随鸡，嫁狗随狗。 In Chinese, this idiom literally means, "When you marry a chicken, you follow the chicken. When you marry a dog, you follow the dog." In other words, once you have married someone, you stick with them. It is a baffling idea to a western mind but no more baffling than the fact that "God chose us in him before the creation of the world" (Ephesians 1:4).

Just like those of us who have sanctified ourselves in faith, these women submit to the circumstance and choices given them. As a result, I see little strife in their spirit, no drive to prove anyone or anything wrong. Mostly a gracious presence radiates out. How many of us can do that?

Their ability to carry on from sunrise to sundown seven days a week without a break has to be one of the most inspiring lessons for me in Shanghai. I know they are not robots. Like us, they long for happiness and enjoy respite too. You see this when Chinese New Year rolls around. The air is full of excitement. People are eager to take a break and go home to see their families. This is the one time they will take off, either one week or for some who travel a long way, they might stretch it to two.

This is their way of life. The markets where they work, the streets which front their shops, are dirty. So confused are we with directions and meet-up places that a friend and I call a place we frequent weekly, "the dirty market". The street cobbler does his job nearby, his old hands still so nimble. Also, out in the alley under the open sky, the barber cuts hair for regular customers. The hands of many of these vendors are swollen from handling wet fish all day or caked with dirt and soil from handling fresh veggies. There is no laziness here. Everyone here is busy at work, finding and having something to do. While the city around them races to build at a feverish pitch, these folks do not find the fastest or easiest way to do things. They simply do what they need to survive.

When I first arrived, I shopped at big western style supermarkets. The "dirty market", a place I resisted going and found so repulsively dirty at first, gradually became a better option in my circumstances. Conveniently located within a ten minute walking distance from my apartment, I didn't have to take a cab or bus to get to a nicer supermarket.

It is not actually dirty by local standards but for those of us expatriates who have bought groceries in less chaotic, cleaner and more orderly places, it was "dirty" by our standards. Hence, the term just stuck. In fact, as the city sprints to build and develop, we found many of these markets tucked away behind the modern façade.

These people and places don't grab headline news. For many Shanghainese, these places and people are a staple of their dynamic city. The women here don't make heads turn with their silky tresses and cool sophisticated air of carrying themselves. Often the words out of their mouth are 今天想买什么？ ("What would you like to buy today?") But they bring me the freshest fish, noodles and eggs. Things I need to feed a family, daily, without fail. I mean, what more could a woman want?

没。赚不到。 ("No, you can't earn enough.") My noodle lady tells me. You can't make enough just sitting in the stall. Her freshly made noodle costs 3.50 RMB for a heavy handful. You have to sell a lot of noodles every day to put some savings away.

先生卖给餐馆、学校、酒店。 ("My husband sells to restaurants, schools, hotels.") So this is where the supply chain begins. The noodles we see in restaurants, which the kids eat in schools, which one enjoys in some of the nicer hotels in town don't often come from a big factory somewhere. The noodles start right here, manufactured at these local "dirty" markets.

"Her husband has full confidence in her and lacks nothing of value." Proverbs 31:11

The other day, I dropped by my veggie seller stall. It was an afternoon. The crowd was thin and we had some time to visit.

不知道为什么。每当清明一到，我想到我父母，我就会哭。好像没做到我的责任似的。("I am not sure why, but come Qingming, I find myself missing my parents. I would cry. I feel I have not done my duty as their child.")

For many Chinese, the Qing Ming Festival is an important event on their social calendar. Some traditional Chinese would return home and perform the grave sweeping duties for loved ones gone before them. For my veggie seller, the ache of not being able to return home to her province was a heart-breaking one.

I put aside my task of looking for vegetables for a minute. Instead, I took on my duty to be a friend for Jesus. I smiled at her, nodded and paused to search inside for a time when I felt such pain. It is a heavy feeling but not one I would toss off carelessly, because Christ has helped me through it.

She soon smiled, centered again. Using her apron she hurried to wipe away some of the remaining tears on her cheeks. In China, there is no Oprah to turn to or Dr Phil around to give useful ideas about how to cope. And certainly no personal God that they know of whom they can talk to. So this is who we are. As followers of a great God, we bring the message of hope and love on behalf of our Savior.

There are many such people to be found in Shanghai. They are hidden behind the alleys and away from the massive concrete and shiny tall buildings. They are often found behind a creaky door, down a dark alley or in a dirty market. They have heartaches and they have husbands. Like us, they are anxious about the paths they see their adult children take. Yet they serve, they sell their vegetables, they sell their meat, they sell their fruit. Their spirit to give their best knocks me out. What a joy it is to be in their spaces. These are truly some of my Shanghai knockout girls.

[Chapter 27] Not Just "Like": the Cost of Following Christ

/Ron/ We were in China for quite a few months before we learned how to get around the internet blocking and access Facebook and other sites from there. Using the VPN was still a hassle, and it made us much less active on social media sites.

Our international church in Shanghai had a series of sermons in 2012 titled "Not a Fan". The point is to not be a casual follower of Jesus nor to be a dismissive non-follower or agnostic. Know what you are committing to or what you are rejecting, but don't just give Christ a "like" and then move on with your life.

There is certainly a cost to following Christ. One of the clearest expressions I got of that came in reading a book written over 75 years ago in a set of difficult circumstances. I'm talking about the life of Dietrich Bonhoeffer during the rise of Hitler's Third Reich in Germany and the book he wrote called *Nachfolge*. It came out in English after World War II as *The Cost of Discipleship*. Bonhoeffer wrote that book with solid conviction and with Biblical and theological clarity. He paid the price for it when he was executed at Flossenburg before he turned 39.

What is the cost of following Jesus? Not mere inconvenience or difficulty, hardship or even suffering. We saw enough of that sort of thing being borne as a daily reality for many Chinese people. The cost of following Jesus is quite simply our life. Life as we know it, as we try to live it, padding and comforting and enjoying ourselves—all of that s laid before Jesus when we respond to his call to follow Him. He gives us true life, lasting joy, grace and blessings that we can get nowhere else. But it comes at the price of our life and the "right" we believe we have to make our own decisions, to call the shots.

In the modern world, we want gadgets, devices and shortcuts that make things easier, faster and simpler. That is what many of us want following Christ to be too.

Following Jesus is not meant to be simpler, easier. If it was, our following of Him really has no power. Because from what I have seen in China, there are so many there who live far harder and more difficult lives than I, and they do not follow Christ. Yet they do what they do with great faithfulness and with great human maturity.

When we can get beyond the "like" and simply obey, to respond to God's call and do what He puts before us without delay and without debate, we will find ourselves on the real path of discipleship.

[Chapter 28] Huang Ayi Teaches Us about Humility

/Angela/ "Mom." My 8 year old looked up from a book he was reading and called out.

"Yes?" I said. I waited for his next question as he stretched his long arms.

"Am I Huang Ayi's young master?" Titus asked.

He was reading *Twice Freed*, a work of historical fiction about a Greek slave.

"In a way, yes. But, you know..."

"Yes, mom. I know."

As a young child I spent a couple of years in Indonesia. My father helped run a textile factory there and in our compound there were many expatriate children. In our household, we had two servants, one to help mom around the house and the other, Sarmi, was our playmate.

In America, we are usually spared the burden to look at people poorer than us up close and personal. In many other cultures, however, maids, domestic helpers or servants from another side of society are part of our lives. As a young kid, I never thought much about them. I just thought they were different from us, the "richer" lot. They appear like Shylock, whose blood we do not realize also bleeds when pricked.

Now that I am a Christian mother, a Christ follower, I suddenly realize the need to see them differently and the responsibility of teaching my children about how to honor Huang Ayi, our household help in China.

A few weeks into the city, I was accosted by a few local women who wanted to be my ayi. One, I remember clearly, wanted to show me all her cooking school credentials. "I know how to take care of you and your family," she assured me, "I know how to bake. I learned it from a German family. They sent me to cooking school." Needless to say, I was rather overwhelmed by the plethora of choices and opinions.

"Things get stolen," others warned me. "They do not practice good hygiene habits. When they wish to quit, it is never face to face but a phone call or text message to tell you 老家有事 ("there are 'matters' to take care of back home"). With more expatriates coming in, they have learned to be picky," I was told. It all made me wonder if ayi help was necessary.

But God found her for me and so in spite of the glitches, I felt I needed to keep myself open and alert to the lessons at hand. A number of my clothes got ruined. I found myself confronted with the question: So which mattered more? The clothes or the person? It was an initial hard lesson. Sometimes when she was in an unhappy mood, the quality of her work showed. Were people not entitled bad days? A few times, she even snapped at me when we first started out. I did not "fire" her but it made me look a lot closer at how I spoke to my family. Is that how I come across?

I had no clue when that chapter would end but I felt it was my duty to learn how to work with her. On matters she was unfamiliar with, I made sure my training instructions were clear and I always made sure she was treated with dignity, including respect from our kids.

"Simple acts, honey," I told my son. "Pick up your stuff so that it makes her easier to clean."

"Greet her, please, when she enters our door."

"Thank her when she is done just before she leaves."

Eventually they learned. Over time the boys and Huang Ayi grew to be quite fond of each other.

你又怎么啦? "What are you crying about this time?" Huang Ayi asked as she entered our house. My eyes are all red. That was how she often found me when I opened the door for her. I was often unable to say what was causing me the sadness. So I cried a lot. In spite of it all, she showed understanding and gave me space. After all, she had traveled her own path like me, leaving her hometown in Anhui for the big city.

"Imagine earning only 300 *kuai* (US$50) a month," she said one day as she wiped the kitchen counter. "It was all we could manage to bring in but we managed." It was her way to speak truth and comfort to me. Huang Ayi often only spoke when I initiated a conversation. Today, though, she took the initiative to comfort another soul.

Gradually she became more than a helper to us. I would find out more about her household. Eventually each week before she leaves, I would find something to give her before she puts on her scarf and heads out the door with my trash. Sometimes it is clothes the boys have outgrown, books or DVDs we no longer need or just extra fruit or vegetables I bought at the market.

A great few months after she worked for us, she came to me with a request if she could work for me on a Sunday instead. It was a great inconvenience to my schedule and our lifestyle habit but I took it on anyway.

It so happened that on Sunday mornings we would make it a practice to partake the Lord's Supper as a family. We would gather at the dining table to have the Lord's Supper for repentance, remembrance, forgiveness, reconciliation and gratitude. On many occasions before that however, we would also find ourselves having to enforce strict discipline on our young boys. Sometimes called for, other times not. The stress of having two very active boys did get the better of us. We would lose our temper and our kids would cry. In those moments of what appears like a family breakdown, I would feel terrible as a parent and worse as a witness for Christ.

One day, enveloped in my own self-pity, I caught her in silent tears as she folded the boys' clothes in their room.

你为什么哭？"Why are you crying?" I asked.

我看你和先生打孩子我心疼。"It hurts me to see you spank your kids," she shared.

While the boys justifiably needed a spank, it did make me pause to examine the way we went about our discipline of our boys. Is that how God looks down at us when we lose our temper and discipline our children in anger? Her non-judgmental response at our flawed parenting gave me fresh understanding at God's

104

patience to let us correct ourselves. So onward we would continue with our lives, our household under her microscope, our family her window to a Christian world. Basically, messed up people who call themselves followers of Christ.

Sometimes I wonder who the real angel is. I used to wrestle with what sort of bad example we might be showing. Heaven forbid that we be a stumbling block for her! But like God, her grace was bigger than ours.

We frequently leave the apartment to let her clean up the place. We would bike, hop on the train to explore the city or get a dessert while she humbly serves us by putting the house in order. Every week, she returns come rain or shine, without any excuse, even with a sick parent or half not well herself, to clean, wash and cook. She saw our faults (big time!) and yet she cast her personal opinion and judgment at the door. Huang Ayi would come faithfully with her attentive service to our home and leave her pleasant contributions behind.

I thought I hired Huang Ayi for household cleaning. But I am seeing it really is just another way for me to understand love in action and full humility demonstrated. It is an opportunity to check my attitude with my kids, to do my mundane housewife job with faithfulness and loyalty, and to sharpen my own understanding of the Christian faith.

[Chapter 29] The Least I Can Do

"Suppose one of you has a servant plowing or looking after the sheep. Will he say to the servant when he comes in from the field, 'Come along now and sit down to eat'? Won't he rather say, 'Prepare my supper, get yourself ready and wait on me while I eat and drink; after that because he did what he was told to do? So you also, when you have done everything you were told to do, should say, 'We are unworthy servants; we have only done our duty.'" Luke 17:7-10

/Angela/ She sells me fresh veggies every week. Because of an old American habit of mine I often buy for the whole week ahead, instead of just for a day or two like the locals. She often throws in garlic and spring onions for free. "Please charge me," I tell her but she insists. Her name is Caiping, the first word "cai" rhyming with the word for "vegetables".

A call-in order and then within an hour, her hubby with a happy baritone voice arrives at my apartment. He rings the bell and says in his sing-song voice, "送菜! " ("Veggie delivery!")

There is not a bone of envy in her. The market where she tends a stall daily gets a fair share of expatriates besides the local maids, which explains the term, "expat market" among my circle of acquaintances. Caiping sells to Polish, American and Taiwanese homemakers, Singaporean and Indian working businessmen. Through us, she gets a window far larger than where she is from in Jiangsu province.

"You work very hard," I say one day. It was a slow day. There was no one she needed to smile at and tell how fresh her produce was. We both had time to visit.

"I have a lot of debt to pay," she replied. I wrinkled my face in confusion. She doesn't strike me as a reckless spendthrift. I looked at her, waiting to hear more.

She tells me as I listen with full attention.

"It is okay," she continues spritely, after a long silent pause. "It will be over soon."

I nodded. I am a talker but in Shanghai, I am learning that if we wait a while, maybe lots of words in long sentences are not necessary. So our eyes meet, and I notice hers are both bright and kind.

I admire her spirit to take on the difficult task at hand, and I tell her so.

I cannot recall the faces of those that stock my produce at Kroger or Walmart or even the Asian supermarket back in Texas. But here in Shanghai, I am led to look deeper. The veggie seller before me is a person, a mom, a woman who loves her son, her family; now I can see it.

In turn, many months later, my husband came home one day with two chiffon red bags. Inside they are stuffed with Chinese candy. Her son had gotten married and she wanted to share her joy with me. I am humbled by her generosity.

These people work all year round, seven days a week. The only off time is during the Chinese New Year holidays, when the greatest mass human migration in the world takes place. The train stations will swell with countless people, and the only way for a foreigner to stay calm is to take cover at home or a vacation outside

107

China to avoid that great migration. Millions of Chinese order their lives that way. It is what keeps this country going: near-continuous, non-stop work.

This spring, my life took on a new routine. I no longer shop for food the way I did in the US. I have gone Shanghainese, I inform my mother. As a result, I frequent the "expat market" where Caiping is less.

When I finally found time to go there again, Caiping was delighted but she also knew from my absence that I was heading into a new chapter. She no longer tells me that she would be happy to deliver. She even poses for me when I ask to take a photo.

I suppose I could just move on, as so many do in this thriving city. People come and go. Shops open and then close their doors before babies learn to crawl. But something in me just wouldn't relent.

"I am not sure I can just give Caiping a Bible," I tell a friend. She understands completely. "I feel I need to do something more. Like pray over it or something," I continue.

Time went by. Finally one day, while packing up my winter clothes, I notice a scarf I had brought here to China. I remember Caiping and thought how she might like this too, something from America.

Still, I had to fight silly thoughts in my head. What will she think? Maybe something like, "Here is this crazy woman who doesn't buy from me anymore. Who keeps forgetting the names of the local veggies. Whose face often draws blank in front of my stall" (if she only knew I was often trying to put together a menu on the fly).

I conclude the only thing to do is to offer her the gift of the Gospel. She helped feed me and my family in this foreign city, so I will bless her with some spiritual food. The Gospel of Mark and John in Chinese, highlighted in places that I find relevant for her. It is the least I can do.

Will she understand?

As I make my way to the market, I suddenly remember a story of how a Bible left as a gift, forgotten and cast aside in the home, was what turned a couple around. From a painful circumstance to a happy new beginning in Christ. Their testimony so inspires me.

So onward I go, discounting no one, not even my veggie seller. I present her a Bible, God's Word. I pray for her to turn to it when questions arise and to hear God's voice speaking to her.

[Chapter 30] On the Road

"By faith Abraham, when called to go to a place he would later receive as his inheritance, obeyed and went, even though he did not know where he was going." Hebrews 11:8

\Ron\ We had been in China a year, getting settled into our adopted home. I had traveled for business several times, but the family had not left Shanghai. I told Angela and the boys that they really should get outside of the city and see more of China. At first, they were not so interested. They didn't want to see more of China; they were already overwhelmed dealing with the part of it represented in Shanghai!

We eventually ventured out further from the city and made trips to nearby Suzhou and then Hangzhou. These are ancient cities with a heritage, places of culture and arts that are less about the brazen commerce of Shanghai. They move at a slightly slower pace. It helped us to see that China is bigger than Shanghai, and that the Chinese cannot be stereotyped or painted in broad brush strokes.

In the spring we had a chance for our first real venture further from the familiar. We joined our church on a weekend trip to rural Anhui province where we delivered baby poultry and basic food items, blankets and other necessities to people in less privileged areas. Some local believers knew who needed the goods and where to steer us to.

Away from the cities, we got to see a different side of China in the wheat fields, bumpy dirt roads, and villages where you saw the very old and very young. The young adults and middle-aged had been drawn to China's cities for work due to economic necessity and the lure of the earning their nest egg.

Though we were bringing gifts to share, the local people were so gracious and hospitable, preparing meals to share with us, welcoming us as honored guests from afar. The warmth and generosity were touching.

I have been in rural places before, talking to simple people who live close to the rhythms of nature. In the Chinese countryside I got back in touch with some basic truths. Jesus came from just such a simple background and was comfortable with people like this. He spoke in uncomplicated teaching stories that drove home deep truths. He dealt with real needs—hunger, illness, death, thirst, shunning, hostile occupation—and met them head-on with power, love and compassion.

I itched to say something meaningful to these people, but what I really needed to do was to keep quiet and listen. I needed to be willing to do what was needed by others, required by the moment, not what my ego wanted.

I saw young children looking for direction and old people who appeared neglected or abandoned, and all that was needed was to show up and to witness, "You are not alone or lost. God cares, He wants you, He will show you the way."

What an eye-opener it is to travel, but only if you have eyes to see new things. I've been struck by how tour groups or individuals often remain insulated when they travel, bringing the comforts of home along, staying well clear of the local culture, foods, people. If you want to see new things, you have to be willing to get uncomfortable, to try something new, and to listen for something other than the familiar.

What we do too often is we manage life, make it comfortable and familiar and predictable and safe. Then

111

in our boredom we try to stimulate or medicate or rejuvenate.

Why not try something different? The lessons of Anhui stayed with us long after we returned to our normal routine. On future trips we went to Nanjing and then to Wuxi and later to Lijiang and Kunming, each time trying to talk and meet with real people and to see something more of what our mission on this earth is. We are surely here for a purpose. We have a message and a witness. Life is about more than comfort, security and luxury. Our riches are meant to be shared or even given up so that we can receive something else, something better.

"Road trip" can be just another indulgence, a self-centered pursuit of what strikes my fancy or pleases me. But it can also be so much more. On the road we can see new things, meet new people, discover things about ourselves that we will never learn if we stay at home. The cross has a road that leads to it. The good news that Jesus shared with us is that once we follow him on that road to the cross, there is another road beyond that leads on. The amazing things we will see and do on that road are only hinted at, but what surprises and miracles are in store!

[Chapter 31] Speak Up

/Angela/ On our first visit to Shanghai during Expo in 2010, I recall reading a story in one of the English dailies there about a worker attempting suicide at a factory in China. It was not one disgruntled worker either, but a symptom of difficult working conditions shared by many of his co-workers.

That article disturbed me. In fact, I can remember enjoying breakfast tea on an otherwise pleasant morning, yet as I read that article I felt the air go out of the room.

The Chinese have a saying: 走头无路. No matter which path you try to take, the efforts are futile. In other words, all roads lead to dead ends. I tried to imagine the feeling of desperation that would drive someone to kill themselves over their work situation, but I couldn't grasp it.

It did get me thinking over Micah 6:8 again.

"And what does the Lord require of you?
To act justly and to love mercy and to walk humbly with your God."

I decided then not to use that company's products. Some people did make remarks about me "not-being-with-it" when I didn't have the latest technology, but that seemed minor compared to the human loss of life. I kept quiet about what I discovered, but I felt in the interest of justice I shouldn't buy those products.

"Speak up for those who cannot speak for themselves,
for the rights of all who are destitute."
"Speak up and judge fairly;

113

defend the rights of the poor and needy." Proverbs 31:8-9

It was a Friday and I was standing in a new school, the system still foreign to me. Suddenly, out of the corner of my eye, I saw the dean of the international division heading my way. Emotions rose within me.

Should I or shouldn't I?

The Chinese way, at least the dignified, educated Chinese way, is " 忍 " (sounds like "run"). Loosely translated, it means to "endure, be longsuffering." It usually looks like tolerance, but it can also lead to passiveness.

But I couldn't "忍" in this matter anymore. Even if it meant confronting someone with whom I needed to be on good terms. Especially when my precious boys are in her school and what she says goes.

Still, I spoke up.

"The cameraman knew what he was doing. If there was a rehearsal, he probably was there. Those close-up shots of her revealing costume were not appropriate on the jumbo screen. The dance moves were too provocative for a school program. Especially when there were also so many young elementary school children among the audience," I gushed out.

One single breath. A moment's silence ensues.

"Well, no one has raised an issue with this. In fact, this is the first time I am hearing it," came her reply.

"Let ME be the first parent to register with the school that I do not approve of it then." My emotions

114

were hot and strong. I am neither proud nor happy that I did not rein in my emotions better. I could have been calmer but I gave vent to indignation.

The dean was visibly stunned that day from our exchange, but later she sent me a most gracious email that showed restraint and seriousness.

I saw something new out of this. All the titles and positions of power mean nothing if you do not speak up for the defenseless, the needy, the young, the innocent, people who do not have a voice.

I used to be overawed by people with big titles or in supposed important positions. That day, the anniversary celebration had thousands of people in the theatre. Many attendees were rich and fairly educated. The fees at this school do not come cheap. And because it was a momentous event in that school, there were also in attendance over 50 important official delegates, all seated in the front row in the performing theatre. They had a full frontal view of these unwholesome dance numbers.

Yet amid this impressive crowd of parents and delegates, no one there made a fuss.

I could imagine my 8 year old blushing in the crowd. He was, and he later told me about it. My children need my protection. They are still poor in using their ability to discern what is appropriate and wrong. They have an inkling, a prompting and they need us as parents to help them confirm the right path. They need our prayers and guidance to know which way to take.

If no voice speaks up, then I will be willing, Lord. Help me to love justice more than saving face.

[Chapter 32] Not Forgotten

/Angela/ 你脱不脱？ ("Will you remove them or not?")

Three gruff men broke the pleasant tourist atmosphere around me with these harsh words to a thirty something local woman. The words were repeated to intimidate her to comply.

I looked up from my bench, slightly alarmed at the audacity of these men. We are on the Nanjing Lu Pedestrian Walk. The woman they were confronting was a street vendor hawking roller skates to the tourists around.

It was a cold winter night. Ron and the boys were at their Monday night Bible Study Fellowship class. I wanted to do some reflecting and writing at the spot where God once found me, a tourist in 2010 then. Where amid the glitter of the lights around, I heard Him awaken my heart to the world beyond my safe and comfortable American suburban life. I wanted so badly that their worship was of the one true God, instead of the glamour and shine all around.

Here I am, two years later, with my family living among the people of Shanghai. After hopping on a bus and riding a subway two stops, I was at the Nanjing Lu Pedestrian Walk in less than 30 minutes.

Now I witness this bullying right before my eyes. I wanted to shout for help. But how do you say it in Chinese? I tried to imagine her going home tonight, her goods gone, bullied and hustled away by these brutish men. There was nothing honorable about how these men treated this woman. But she is not forgotten.

Several times in my suburban life I had been able to practice loving mercy. In marriage, raising kids and in relationships with people, I learned to walk humbly with my God. But to act justly? I tried to do things honorably and with integrity in every aspect of my life but to act when injustice has been done? Acting justly was an area in my life I had little exposure to and practice in.

(Journal Entry: Nov 2, 2012)

Woe is me but do not walk on by.

When I saw him, I crossed the road so that I do not have to see him. This leper full of scarred skin sitting on the entrance of Laojie at Yuyuan.

I hurried along, quickened my steps. I need to get my house shoes. No time to lose. Kids coming home soon. This errand, more like an excursion, required me to negotiate the crazy traffic in Shanghai. But I signed up to teach kids' class at church this week with the family. I am leading the family and a bunch of kids... How can I walk on by? That would be like teaching a Bible lesson without making the effort to live it out.

What would Jesus do? My conscience does not allow me to ignore the leper.

I crossed back again. I looked for him. I gave him a mooncake, a mid-Autumn Festival treat. More importantly, eye contact. A return of his human dignity. He looks at me and smiled.

So here I am in China, thankful for the opportunity to see amazing views of the Bund day or night. Learning to live with grace like the locals do through all the cold, foggy skies that few visitors see.

I see the suffering, the poverty here, in everyday Shanghai: on my way to get groceries, buy my bread, find my house shoes. But first, I see *my* suffering first.

(Journal Entry: March 19, 2013)

A man begs for money on the train. I am tired. I refused to make eye contact, like the rest of the commuters. Then I soften up and lower my defenses. In my moment of hesitation, he notices and lingers in front of me. "You'll be rich," he says. His empty promise isn't what sways me. It is God's Spirit whispering to my heart. "I have not forgotten him."

I am sure I have no spare change, remembering I gave my last bit to Markus for his lunch money at school.

He finally walks away. My stop was coming up. I got up and walked toward him. I rummaged my purse and actually found some coins. I saw his back, still begging for money. I have seen the blind, the crippled on Line 9, begging for money. Nobody shoos them off or reports them, even in this place where there's always a set of eyes on you. I think we all knew deep in our hearts they are to be pitied, to be shown compassion.

I wanted to give him coins and also say, "Jesus saves!" But my courage fails me. I find myself gagged. I am the one stopping myself. How on earth did Peter find this boldness to say, "Silver or gold I do not have, but what I have I give you. In the name of Jesus Christ of Nazareth, walk." (Acts 3:6)

I want that boldness, to lift this beggar from his darkness. Yet I have little courage and wished for a spokesman like Aaron and Hur (Genesis 17:12) by my side.

The work to be a light for Jesus is often difficult.

"I see my suffering first." I am wretched. Just like the apostle, Paul. Sometimes I do what I can. And sometimes quite frankly, I don't.

118

I see a lot of distressing poverty here, even in modern Shanghai. You can only imagine the poverty in the rural areas in this country. As a follower of Christ, I can't just do church week after week and think it is enough, no matter how deeply rooted I think I am with God.

I never saw my good forture or blessedness until I came to China.

"Can you imagine?" says Janet, a dear sister of mine, "What would happen if our forefathers never left China?"

"We could be working as maids and never have the opportunities that we now have." She is a Singaporean who went to live in the US several years and now lives in Shanghai. We still cannot comprehend the grace that brought us thus far but we are in awe of it.

So this is what a number of Christian expats here do in a foreign city. They deliberately buy at "dirty" markets so that that "wealth is shared with these folks as well", as one tells me. Young children are moved to give money to street side beggars.

Whenever an expatriate family leaves, clothes are gathered up and given to the veggie sellers and meat vendors. Some buy electric blankets for their a-yi's, the maids.

A few extraordinary ones even adopt orphans and foot the bills of all their medical surgeries.

In China, the "forgotten" are all here, nowhere less important than the curious tourists or the well-to-do Shanghainese that this city receives daily. They are all

119

here. And definitely not forgotten by a God who trudged the lonely path all the way to the cross, followed not too far behind by a people who love following Him.

"How beautiful on the mountains are the feet of those who bring good news, who proclaim peace, who bring good tidings, who proclaim salvation, who say to Zion," Your God reigns!"   Isaiah 52:7

[Chapter 33] Money and Security

"Therefore I tell you, do not worry about your life, what you will eat or drink; or about your body, what you will wear. Is not life more than food, and the body more than clothes? Look at the birds of the air; they do not sow or reap or store away in barns, and yet your heavenly Father feeds them. Are you not much more valuable than they? Can any one of you by worrying add a single hour to your life?

... So do not worry, saying, 'What shall we eat?' or 'What shall we drink?' or 'What shall we wear?' For the pagans run after all these things, and your heavenly Father knows that you need them. But seek first his kingdom and his righteousness, and all these things will be given to you as well. Therefore do not worry about tomorrow, for tomorrow will worry about itself. Each day has enough trouble of its own."
Matthew 6:25-27, 31-34

/Angela/ How could you not talk about money in a place like Shanghai?

One hundred years ago Shanghai was *the* place to be for making and spending money. The "Paris of the East" they called it, a magnet for the business people and bankers, crime lords, colonialists, and developers of that age. From 1940-1990, war, politics and economics shifted the action elsewhere.

After China's reform and opening up in the 1990's Shanghai started rebuilding. The east coast of the Huangpu River—Pudong—was developed at a breakneck pace and gained an conic new skyline within a decade.

Whether you are downtown in the financial and banking district or living on the outskirts, in this city, the preoccupation to make money takes center stage. It draws people from near and far to the city. Stay a little while and you'll soon notice that the content of many conversations around here is about money. It doesn't matter the age, the class or the location. People here like making deals.

Jesus talked a lot about money too. I think many Christians missed (or pretended they didn't notice?) some of his teachings. I am still learning to accept what He has to say on it.

"No one can serve two masters. Either he will hate the one and love the other, or he will be devoted to the one and despise the other. You cannot serve both God and Money."
Matthew 6:24

The grass withers, the flowers fade but the word of the Lord stands forever. (Isaiah 40:8).

This is the truth yet we chase, seek and pursue everything but God. Me included. At the same time, we sometimes snicker at the blatant expressions of *others* chasing money or using it for indulgence, but when I look closely at the content of my many journals, I notice money has been an overriding concern for me as well.

I had made it clear to my husband that unless there was a base income I wasn't willing to move the family to Shanghai. But as God would have it, a few months after we arrived, we found ourselves in a situation where the job providing the steady income went away and we were thrown onto living off of freelance work. It was a very hard first year.

I definitely was angry. I also had the feeling of being left alone, cast out and forgotten even though I was very sure we were commissioned to go to Shanghai. Would I reject God just because life is hard?

122

What use is a God who doesn't bless me with stuff I need? Why hold on to faith?

In our first year here, there were several occasions when I found myself out of ideas on how to put food on the table after the essential bills were paid. I have had hard times before but that year in Shanghai felt especially so, maybe because we were in a foreign land and food I usually bought was row twice or sometimes three times as expensive as back home. I felt sick in my stomach that I couldn't provide meals and maintain life as it was before. Recipes had to be changed. Alternative sources were needed to keep the family well fed.

There was nothing saintly about my prayers. How do I go on from here, Lord? How do I feed my family, Lord? The lost around me as well as reaching out to be their friend was the last thing on my mind.

Yet if there is anything we are to learn about clinging on to our very identities as Christians is that we are admitting to the world that we need the Lord to provide. But how many of us would make deliberate moves like that? Usually it is when we are edged out of our jobs, teetering on death, at the end of our rope that we kneel at the foot of the Cross for help. In China, I was asked to really look at: Would I really, really trust the Lord to provide from now on?

The kitchen at our apartment was hard to work in. In the winter, food put out on the counter to thaw would stay frozen all day. The kitchen faucet kept coming loose and in the end I just quit calling the resident plumber. There was no utility room. The area where the small washer and dryer sat was so small that only one person could fit in there. Mold grew on the walls like weeds in springtime until a friend of mine and I worked together to kill it with the strongest bleach we could find in the market.

Over time, the whining grew less as I learned to gather up myself in this strange new place and cook for the family. Of course, on occasion, I was discouraged by the quality of water and food here. But I figure I could be resilient like the many locals here. In due time, with God's guidance, I gained a new facility on how to shop for groceries my Shanghai way.

Before Shanghai, I had in the undercurrents an erroneous belief. I would call it a sin now. It was the idea that if I had the perfect kitchen or house or kids or husband, then truly everything would be okay. Although I knew cognitively these were not true, and I worked hard not to buy into these illusions, it often *felt* true, and it was an open door of discontent that I did not shut completely out of my life.

For a great number of years, another sin that stunted me from doing a lot of things for the Kingdom had been this: God, I don't have enough. Please wait till I have enough, then I will do, go and act.

And as my husband once asked me, before the kids came and before his hair showed traces of gray: How much exactly is enough? When will we know it? For years, I ran around in that vicious cycle.

"But my people have exchanged their Glory for worthless idols.
Be appalled at this, O heavens,
and shudder with great horror," declares the Lord,
"My people have committed two sins:
They have forsaken me, the spring of living water,
and have dug their own cisterns,

broken cisterns that cannot hold water." Jeremiah 2:11-13

Growing up in cosmopolitan Singapore, I was exposed to some of the finest things in the world. Like many urban dwellers, it was not difficult to develop a fancy for the fine things in life. Later on in the US, when I joined the ranks of the middle class, I found myself soon in, I am not proud to admit, the same preoccupation. Even though I know an eye on worldly things is a broken cistern that does not hold satisfying water, I enjoyed every bit of the short-lived pleasure.

I soon saw through God's grace how flawed my thinking was in equating God's goodness with overflowing "blessings" and abundant prosperity. Life isn't good just because the statements tell me I have plenty of money. Life isn't pitiful just because there is hardly any. Once and for all, I had to work at deciding that our financial accounts no longer have the final authority about the mood of my life.

I still find myself running ahead, wanting to know how to make ends meet, how to pay for all the wants that feel like necessities. The more I plan and consider the options, the more anxious I become, not sure where to turn, which path to take. So I discipline myself to stop this thinking and instead turn to the training God's word provides us. He *will not* fail. He loves forever and will provide.

In Shanghai, here in Lujiazui, where some of the world's finest retailer shops are found, it dawned on me that maybe I was a very good church-going Christian but not a very good witness for Christ. Be all poured out like Him? I did that for family and some close friends but for the world? What did I really know about that?

I could not see it then. A veil of darkness was over me. If He is really all I want, why is it so important that I snag a good deal on things and pour much energy over them? Why do I look at pretty catalogues or let eye candy be a preoccupation? But they look good! I tell myself. How am I not like my children? I want the stuff, mom, it's fun! Very mature indeed.

"We live in a competitive culture where envy is the indoor sport of Americans—the envy trap."   -- Rick Warren

I certainly did not know I was engaged in an envy sport. All I know is I didn't like it if I think somebody had something better than I did. I am not sure if it is what my soul desires. All this stuff and the work to maintain it, keep it up, improve, revamp or upgrade it whenever the mood, season or holiday sales determine it.   This preoccupation did not draw me closer to Christ though, much less hunger for Him. That much I know for sure.

The fact is some of us are indeed given much materially. In Shanghai, many expatriate families come to the city with the provision of full time maids, chauffeurs, private schools and villas or apartments with breathtaking views of the Bund. When you have much, will you declare that "Jesus Saves" or is He a sideline trophy you happened to collect on your way to success?

Will you share Christ and be His light for so many who have never heard the name, "Jesus"? The name that when spoken sends demons flying, heals the sick and restores the soul to complete wellness. It seems a foolish exercise to wonder how others find so much money to spend. Do I bring this silly channel of envy and continue it in China? Or worse, be upset that I do not have a full-time ayi to cook my daily meals, do all my

126

laundry and a chauffeur for my beck and call? Perspectives change. New insights come. God is gracious. Enough of the silly wanting already! Jehovah-Jireh. The Lord provides.

I have what I need, in the moment that I need it. I am also able to enjoy many things. In the moment that God is gracious to give. Not only does He provide, He brings me to worlds I never consider going on my own. His world is larger and has so much more color. Yes, Lord. I follow You.

[Chapter 34] God's Provision

"Do not conform any longer to the pattern of this world, but be transformed by the renewing of your mind." Romans 12:2

/Angela/ Six months into our stay in Shanghai, there's this entry from one of my journals (March 2012): "Very strange. Every time we do the Lord's work, availing ourselves to meet and be with Christians here, we receive money deposited into our bank accounts. Previously, 10K RMB. Today, 4800 RMB into Ron's account."

I have worn my red Lands' End parka for two winters now. Friends spot me easily in a crowd. My boys look for the red parka when they need to find me. I am getting tired of it even though it still works. My excuse? All that smoke, oil and grime of the city. And also that vain pride of wanting something new to wear. Would I take my very durable Lands End red parka back into my pristine American closet and home when I return? Will a good hot wash be enough to remove all the memories of dirt and smoke I had experienced here? What about the cleansing I need to do inside? Isn't that more important?

In Shanghai, I realize it's the happy fervor I need to cultivate, this pursuit of Christ. To be sure, the opportunities to serve back in the US are plenty, just as family and church there remind us. But we are stubborn. We know the need out there is bigger. Moreover, God has equipped us with special gifts and talents for this work. I think, though, God brought us here first not so much for the good we aspire to do but so we can know Him even more deeply. From a worldly point of view, it seemed to make no logical sense. But that is how God pursues us. Through difficult times, broken relationships

128

and arduous intercontinental moves. He so desires that I know Him and dwell in His presence. It is a desire I am still unraveling and taking in.

Certainly the training and knowledge transfer that Ron does in the marketplace is very useful. I have found a way to be available and be a blessing to people here as well. But the whole exercise in willingness amounts to this: to know how deeply He loves us and desires us to know Him even deeper. This amazing God, ruler over everything, wants to know me, us, you.

When we said yes, we assumed God's favor would be one continuous flow upon us. The money did come, the seeds sown and the joy of receiving the reward of being paid for work done, it is all a blessing. But He wanted something even more delightful - our hunger for Him. Until we were thoroughly stripped down, nothing to get, no one to help us, when we saw perhaps the only way is to find ourselves back to the Cross. That is the treasure.

Today, we count our blessings not because we have conquered this city in possessing all the things this city promises. I could get more things if I work harder or have the 关系 (guanxi-right connections). I have tasted the goodness of being all emptied out and letting God act. The more I let Him, I find more of myself to empty: my impatience, my lack of belief, my lack of trust.

One experience in getting a clothes dryer spoke to me in an especially powerful way.

"Show us (me) your Glory, Lord. Lord, please show your Glory by providing a new dryer to us effortlessly. Please give us a new dryer, Father. Please, Lord." (Journal Entry, November 2011)

"HE DID!" (Journal Entry, January 2012)

"You are the God who performs miracles; you display your power among the peoples." Psalms 77:14. Five months into the city, I finally could dry my clothes using a dryer instead of hanging them over dining chairs to dry!

This moment I am writing here by the Huangpu River. An old man from Jiangsu who I don't know plants himself next to me and is so curious about what I am doing and my life. It is not uncommon in China that people watch and "intrude" into my space in a way that Americans would find uncomfortable. I also want to keep my distance and be private. But he really wants to know. Will I share or brush him off?

I asked him if he knew Jesus. He said he had never heard of Him. I tell him I believe in Jesus. He looked at me, not sure if I came from Mars and asked if I worked. I am writing, this is my work. I will need to buy groceries for the house. That is a lot of work too! I comfort my boys and point them to Jesus when they get all confused outside. It does pay. Yet he cannot see it.

I tell him the Lord provides and I feel silly saying it. But it is true. God has provided and provides still. My mother, in a flash of anxiety, asked and was worried about our well-being in a conversation several months ago. Finally in a moment at which I had enough of such doubt, I raised my voice above the raucous and asked her, "Mom, I have been away, almost 20 years from Singapore. Stop for a minute. Has the Lord not provided?"

That truth snaps her out of her anxiety. It is true. She has seen me take her to some incredible places and enjoy some very marvelous things and she has witnessed the challenges and difficulties I faced out away from home. Yet the Lord has carried me through. Today, she knows the Lord watches out for me. And so when I am weak, forgetting, she reminds me. Grace comes full circle. I am grateful.

"Those who cling to worthless idols forfeit the grace that could be theirs." Jonah 2:8.

Months later, we received a stable salary again plus extra commissions from work delivered. Not only could we save and wire money out of the country, we found ourselves in a spot where we could give to others as well. Like secret agents, we give away packets of money in envelopes. We give to those we know are doing the Lord's work. They know what to do with the money. This was an example first given to us by our very good friends, Anna and Joseph. We now practice that habit.

Lord Jesus, Savior of my life. God, Maker of Heavens and Earth. Holy Spirit, the power to cleanse and heal completely. Take control. Reign over me. You know I will always need money to pay for gas, put food on the table, pay school fees. I ask that you give me ample enough where I will not worry where my next meal would come from. I also ask that you give me enough where I can say "yes" to generosity. Forgive me when I forget to ask what to do for others when I have much. Teach me to always trust, always believe that there is plenty and more than enough. Whether it is money, wisdom or love. And when there isn't, simply to pray and ask for it. Jehovah-Jireh. The Lord provides. In Jesus' Name, I pray, Amen.

"He is no fool who gives what he cannot keep to gain what he cannot lose." Jim Elliot (1927–1956)

[Chapter 35] Scale a Wall with God

"With your help I can advance against a troop; with my God I can scale a wall." Psalm 18:48.

/Angela/ "How are you, Markus' and Titus' mom?" the text message reads. "I am wondering if you are free this Friday at 1 pm? I would love to chat with you."

Immediately my armor goes up. The head of the elementary school international division doesn't just text you to have a casual chat.

"About?" I texted back.

"About how your kids are doing in Chinese class and other matters."

So I called her straight away. No more texting.

老师，你好。 ("Hello, Teacher.") In China, you need to show respect and so you call someone "Teacher" or "Master" even if they don't hold class. This includes your cab driver, chauffeur and even your plumber.

马克思和泰德思妈妈，你好。 ("How are you, Markus and Titus' mom.")

孩子有事吗？ ("Is there anything amiss with the boys?") Not missing a beat, I dove straight to the point and asked if the kids were alright. No need for any delicate social pleasantries here.

孩子没事。只想问孩子进展如何？ ("The boys are okay. I just want to find out how they are progressing along.")

132

我们两个孩子都好。一切没事。谢谢老师关心。
("Our kids are doing well. All is well. Thank you, Teacher, for your concern. ")

"That is good to know," she tells me. "I would like to meet you though and see if everything is alright." This woman teaches class, runs a division and looks like a rising star in the public school system. She wants to meet even when I inform her that my kids would no longer be at the school this fall?

Except for a few marvelous individuals I know, the business of telling the truth is hard. Very much like constipation.

So here is the truth. This department head, she calls because I have refused to give in to the school's private vendor for English classes. The manager in charge of this account had been texting me and I have stayed resolute in my decision not to pay the extra fees.

The English classes are taught by a foreign teacher and outsourced to a private vendor. The school's intent is to boost the English standard, which it probably does. We discovered it wasn't any help to our boys and was in fact dumbing down their language.

At first, I used my western-trained style of using empirical evidence to persuade the school to let us have a choice in this. They listened with politeness and patience but were unmoved. Our purpose of having them in China is to learn Chinese, so they were allowed to work on Chinese assignments in English class as long as they took the English tests and passed them.

Apparently, however, we were still expected to pay the extra fee for the English language class even if our boys were not participating in class.

"If you do not pay, then others may follow. Where do we put the kids who do not need the extra English classes? We can't simply let them sit around outside class."

I tried to protest with more human reasoning. She would have none of it.

So I stop talking. I pray. "Spirit of holy conviction, help me in this."

"If there is a student in your school that is in financial need," I found my voice rising with supernatural strength, "Please, let me know. I will," still trying to believe my words that came after, "give my money there. But I'm not giving money to support this private English language school."

Silence. Finally, she understood. It is not about money but convictions.

这样子，让我和他们商量吧。("So it's like that. Let me talk to them about it.")

I never heard from her since. I took it as a sign that God helped me scale another impossible wall in China. In all encounters, it seems, the real test is not about changing or convincing others, but the transformation of myself—the courage to speak up and do the right thing.

"In the beginning was the Word, and the Word was with God, and the Word was God." John 1:1

Since God had delivered me with the right words in my moment of need, I was determined to donate the money and not hang on to it. I gave the first half of the money away fairly easily. Then I got stuck. It would have made things easier if the teacher had called back and asked for the money as a donation. It would have provided an easy way to be held accountable. Instead, I investigated a few charities—all very worthy—but I pursued none of them. Life went on and I did nothing more.

I feel the presence of the Lord has left me, I tell my friend Janet one day. She hits the panic button even though normally she is cool and calm. She wants to know what is going on.

"What happened?" she asked.

"I think I am supposed to honor God on something I had promised some time back," I explained.

I told her the story. "I need to give the rest away. So, would you join me in checking out this group?" I asked. Janet has a car and driver.

"So you want to prequalify the need?" she asked.

There I was, thinking myself so smart, to find this easy solution. But that question immediately stops me. I really do not know who deserves the money using my human eyes and heart. I do need to go back to the drawing board with God again.

In my journal, amid several things, I wrote the following words, "testify to His goodness".

A day later, I received an email forwarded to me. A few expatriate women here have taken upon themselves to raise 200,000 RMB for a new babe in Christ for her cancer treatment.   I knew immediately that was the cause to which the remaining money was to go.

I still do not understand why it is this cause and not others.   I knew my other contacts better.   But doing things that do not make sense seems to be what I am to do these days. A flurry of email connections were made and followed up.   I found myself forwarding alongside the money this verse to my unknown sister in Christ undergoing cancer treatment.

"The Lord himself goes before you and will be with you; he will never leave you nor forsake you. Do not be afraid; do not be discouraged." Deuteronomy 31:8

Slowly, I think I am starting to see. Wall scaling is not so much about claiming personal victories or be pleased with one's ability to conquer them.   Hard tasks are many and they are but a chance for God to work with me and in me, to help me pick the right ones to scale and to scale them with His wisdom and power.

[Chapter 36] Hello? Hello! Hello, God.

/Angela/ Loud firecrackers were set off as our church group arrived at this old folks' home. The roads in the rural country of China are not smooth. Dirt tracks are plenty. Our group was big and drew attention from the locals. Unsure how to behave, we entered the courtyard quietly and offered smiles at the people watching us. In a huge white washed building there were individual rooms, each occupied by an old person.

This retirement home was for many of the old folks in the village. We were told that many of their family and relatives have gone into the city for work. Here, in the village, these folks lived alone in small individual rooms. We came to bring them cooking oil and essential supplies for the months ahead.

I ventured upstairs and found an old man by the end of the corridor. He was alone, a few sparse strands of white hanging down from his chin. I walked closer and hesitated. He wasn't friendly. I wasn't sure how to proceed. Like so many, this was a man who had worked hard all his life, tending the fields, taking care of farm animals. I wasn't so sure how to feed a sow I saw on our way here that looked almost five times my size. After a lifetime of toil, this man now lives alone in the old folks' home.

Should I or should I not? So, I did.

I gave him a copy of my handmade journals. It was meant for a child but it felt right to extend the gift to him. I tried imagining what went through his mind as he held my gift, moving his old fingers slowly around it. Not sure how to give him space, I decided to peer in and survey his room. A rusty wash basin. A creaky wooden bed with an equally unsteady table. It was a room of an old simple farmer.

I drew the green spring trees lining the walls of the courtyard on the journal. We surveyed the scene before us and I showed him what I saw. He looked at me, then at the journal, at the trees and then at me again.

"He's deaf," said a helpful man who came along and offered his opinion.

"It's ok," I said, and continued to show him how I'd paste stickers of frogs on his blank journal book if it were mine. I watched him study my stickers with the greatest curiosity and I suddenly realized he probably hadn't played with such fun things before.

He smiled. I smiled. We both relaxed.

After a few moments, I waved him goodbye. It was time to go.

He waved me goodbye, slowly and as gently his old age could allow.

The grains have been delivered, so have the cooking oil, the blankets and every loving gift we thought we could pass on. The crowd had gotten larger; the community had come to watch. The courtyard was abuzz with people, getting ready to sing. Out of the corner of my eye, I saw him coming down the stairs.

That old man on the second floor at one of the last rooms further back, had finally decided. He wanted to be a part. Out in the courtyard, a group of Christians sing. God's heart shines into this forgotten old folks' home in the middle of nowhere. Like him, I reckon it is never too late to join broken community and open one's heart to holy Grace.

[Chapter 37] Christ Came for the Diors and Chanels Too

"The important thing is that in every way, whether from false motives or true, Christ is preached. And because of this, I rejoice." Philippians 1:18

/Angela/ I have been incredibly blessed. On our first Sunday in Shanghai, my husband's business partner invited the whole family for lunch at an expensive buffet lunch at the Waldorf Astoria. Not just me and Ron but the whole group - our kids plus my mom who was visiting us. It was one expensive lunch, especially when the boys chose to eat croissant mainly when caviar and French champagne were free flow, but still the generous giver didn't mind one bit.

One of my friend's chauffeur is a college kid who enjoys giving us tidbits of information about his society. Oh, a 爆发户 (nouveau rich) drives a Porsche. That's the latest these days. What about a Bentley? Oh, that's driven by a 富二代 (second generation wealth). The Maserati and Ferrari are also favored by that group, he tells us. They sleep during the day but they come alive at night in the pubs on HuaiHai Lu.

My friend's driver makes a turn as we continue to listen to his social commentary. The 官二代 (government officials' children) however like to drive the Audis. Now, you wouldn't want to drive a BMW convertible, he says laughingly. It's a sure giveaway. It's even called a 二奶车 (second wife car) and it's definitely for a 小白脸 (gigolo).

Shanghai is indeed home and a pleasure place to many Chinese with much money. Husbands, boyfriends, fathers make fast easy money and many like to spend it or show it off here. If they so happen to be out-of-towners from other provinces, they can easily find classy respite at the Ritz on both sides of the HuangPu River.

Such eye-popping wealth can cause subtle resentment in folks like me though. It is an easy card Satan uses to play on me, his way to make me forget that behind all this incredible wealth lies a soul who is loved by God and needs God all the same.

The other day I was riding an elevator down and making small talk with a local Chinese I had just met. Into the elevator entered a well-coiffed lady, elegantly chic. Her porcelain face was flawlessly white and she wore accessories worth several months' of a regular white collar paycheck.

It took restraint to not stare. I focused my conversation on my new contact. She overheard what I was sharing and immediately turned around and joined in. "So, you know of a prayer meeting group here?" she asked.

Startled, I said yes and mentioned that she could find one gracious hostess on the 45th floor in the very block where she resided.

讲中文吗? ("Chinese-speaking?")

Unfortunately, I said, it is conducted in English. But if she is interested in a Chinese speaking group, I can introduce one to her.

"What kind are they?" She asked.

"What kind are they? Sorry, I am afraid I do not understand."

"Like where are they from?"

What? Is this a trick question? I wonder.

"Shanghai, Zhejiang, all over, I guess." What exactly was I supposed to say?

She shook her head rigorously and said, "No."

"Oh, I see! You are looking for a Chinese speaking group with foreign passports!" my acquaintance helped me understand her request.

She smiled, said yes, half coy yet still earnest.

Encounters like that make me immediately annoyed. It seems to go against my sense of what Christian community should be. James 2 assumes rich and poor are together in the same meeting. But since she is not my child or my husband, I do not raise my voice.

Aren't these also people for whom Jesus came? For Zacchaeus, Festus and King Agrippa? Yes, Jesus can be her friend. Others can be her friends. Why not connect her with others?

I asked the two ladies of this posh residence to exchange numbers. "I am sure the hostess can find a group that fits you," I said.

She is happy. The two banter and move on, talking like the two on Emmaus Road while I go upstairs again to retrieve my forgotten umbrella on this rainy day.

As much as I want to judge this woman, Christ came for her too. This is one of my big realizations--and a frustration too. God called me to serve the poor, but not them alone. He, for His own reasons, also wants to save the rich and well-off, and he has asked me to witness to them too. I am not materially rich or wealthy. Nothing especially commends me for serving this group, except that I don't rule them out. And the gospel is for the rich and well-heeled. God's mercy triumphs over judgment (James 2:13). The scandal of it all!

"Here there is no Greek or Jew, circumcised or uncircumcised, barbarian, Scythian, slave or free, but Christ is all, and is in all." Colossians 3:11

[Chapter 38] Walking with Our Kids

"Impress them on your children. Talk about them when you sit at home and when you walk along the road, when you lie down and when you get up." Deuteronomy 6:7.

/Angela/ "How do you hunger for God's Word?" my ten year old son Markus asks. He is sincere and wants to know. I do not know quite what to say. I have to give up my delusions of thinking that a one-time response is enough. So, with great patience, I teach once more.

"It starts with practice," I say. "I write out Bible verses that speak to me. Before I know it, I write them so that I can meditate on it." It helps that we studied medieval times together. We had learned about monks diligently writing words from the Bible in their most focused hearts in a scriptorium. Their example becomes our model. Our method is not much different from them. We turn away from distractions and we write out God's Word.

My spirit though needs more changing. I have sworn to not punish my kids with Bible verse writing when they misbehave. But I have. Because of that, I have done wrong.

I let that mistake rule me rather than asking God for help, to wash away the wrong spirit. "God, your Spirit in me, please. Guide me in the teaching and learning of the Word together with my children."

"No one lights a lamp and puts it in a place where it will be hidden, or under a bowl. Instead they put it on its stand, so that those who come in may see the light. Your eye is the lamp of your body. When your eyes are healthy, your whole body also is full of light. But when they are unhealthy, your body

144

also is full of darkness. See to it, then, that the light within you is not darkness. Therefore, if your whole body is full of light, and no part of it dark, it will be just as full of light as when a lamp shines its light on you." Luke 11:33-36

I have seen it. I give God praise. How peace, joy and wisdom grow in strength in the family, among us when I lead in the right Spirit. I am humbled by their insights and then wonder why I don't do this often.

I examine this popular verse again. Deuteronomy 6:7. Did I remember the previous line?

"Love the Lord your God with all your heart and with all your soul and with all your strength. These commandments I give you today are to be upon your hearts." Deuteronomy 6:5.

Therein lies the problem. I, the parent, need to get this first. No amount of coing the right things, implementing the right tips from the right books, listening to the right counsel, watching the right examples will turn my boys into sons of God. It starts with my heart, my everything given over to God. This is walking humbly with God.

Love the Lord my God with all my heart, all my soul and all my strength.

Holy Spirit, take over. Come, please.

Jesus, nail my shortcomings to the Cross. Come, please.

You are my example. You are my Savior. Teach me how to love the Father.

[Chapter 39] Spiritual Amnesia

/Angela/   There is a security guard in our apartment neighborhood whose spirit to learn inspires me. The odds are clearly stacked against him. The opportunity to go far in school when he was young was missed, like so many during the tumultuous years of the Cultural Revolution.

Years later though, when we met, his desire to learn new things never stopped. Our family calls him 朱保安 (Zhu Bao'an) which literally means, "Security Guard Zhu" (sounds like "Jew") as our way to distinguish him from the rest of the guards and show him respect.

I found it peculiar that I would be noticed when I first set up house in our China neighborhood. I had spent a great number of years doing many things myself, just like many Americans. I would pull up in our driveway, unload my groceries, herd my noisy boys back into the house all on my own. On occasion, there might be casual chats between neighbors but no one would come and help me carry in groceries even if my body was battered from fatigue and a kid had just spilled Goldfish crackers in the minivan.

In Shanghai however, the frequent greeting from Zhu Bao'an changed all that. I was to be reminded that there were really living people around me, whether I care to acknowledge them or not.

Perhaps we were such an oddity, but Zhu Bao'an would regularly leave his sentry post to come greet us.

"Markus! Titus! How are you?" He would yell out in his halting broken English, every word an exclamation.

Sometimes he would hasten his steps to help us open the lobby door while we were fumbling for our keys.

Unlike other fancier apartment neighborhoods in our area, our guards were expected to stay at their posts and only respond to us when we asked for it. The fact that he bothered to greet us, often hurried toward us and wanted to open the door for us showed me that he really wanted to make contact. For Zhu Bao'an, his desire to learn a few English phrases was strong.

When we met he knew how to say, "Tank you."

你这么讲 "不客气" ("How do you say, "You're welcome"?")

"You," I said. Zhu Bao'an was all ears and repeated after me slowly.

"...are...welcome," I continued. He followed slowly, trying to work his Chinese tongue into the right vowels.

"Wel...." He struggled and paused.

"...come," I encouraged. But silence met me back.

"是个"k"声音," I offered. ("It's a "k".)

"kkkkkk," he finally repeated after me. And after a short while, he ventured further and said, "Come".

My boys watched the whole situation. In time too, they also became his tutor. I have often thought about my encounters with Zhu Bao'an.

Here is a man who wants to learn a few simple English phrases badly. How badly do I want to know the Bible? How badly do I desire to know God's heart? Perhaps that is why Zhu Bao'an appeared in my life.

When I first became a Christian, I too was an eager student of the Word. I wanted to know everything there was to learn about the Bible. Wednesday midweek, Sunday Bible classes and sermons were not enough. I attended any seminar possible, asked my teachers myriads of questions and studied materials that deepened my understanding of the Book.

Somewhere along the shuffle of faithful church attendance, I moved from an eagerness to learn to polite listening to critiquing what I heard and saw. I found myself more concerned over what to eat after service or what to wear on Sundays. The sermons were great to hear. I listened, I applied, but nothing so great that I would alter my world completely for radical change. In other words, somewhere in the coming and going, I began to suffer from spiritual amnesia. I had forgotten what the Message was all about.

Volunteering at church, ministering to widows and singles, choosing to be a home-maker mother were some things I did. But did I also realize that I, a follower of Christ, have the power to send "Satan falling like lightning from heaven" (Luke 10:18)?

In Shanghai, like so many places real and online, there are many pretty and interesting things to look at, do and talk about. The city draws people both from within China and from outside like a magnet.

Expatriates like us can get tired of these easily and so many head out of Shanghai on a high speed train or plane to explore other parts of China or fly off to other countries in the region. In less than three hours, you can find yourself in Hong Kong, Taiwan, Korea or Japan, or head for the beaches in Thailand and the Philippines.

As long as man has an appetite of desires and passions, there is no short supply to satisfy it. My dear friend and mentor, Anna, a fashion designer tells me her last words from her visit with us in Shanghai.

"Get behind me, Satan! You do not have in mind the things of God, but the things of men." (Mark 8:33)

Zhu Bao'an keeps it simple. There is only one goal. For him, it is to learn English. For Christians, it is to love the Lord.

There is a movement among some in China to be God's light here on earth. I believe the same is happening elsewhere as well.

People deserve more than just a good English lesson or two or the label of "nice Christians" in our midst. People need to know that there truly is a God who is alive and is at work in all of us who say we follow Him. It is a precious testimony we have and we become a living Bible for people when we let God speak through us.

[Chapter 40] Who is My Neighbor?

"But he (expert in the law) wanted to justify himself, so he asked Jesus, "And who is my neighbor?".......
"Which of these three do you think was a neighbor to the man who fell into the hands of robbers?"
The expert in the law replied, "The one who had mercy on him."
Jesus told him, "Go and do likewise." Luke 10:29, 36-37.

/Angela/ 你们关门可以轻一点吗？ "Could you close your door quietly?" a woman with curlers in her hair popped out of her apartment and asked. She must have noticed my surprised glare.

我妈妈年老了。 "My mother is getting along in age," she softened up and explained. 有心脏病。 "She has heart problems," she elaborated.

I pretended to understand but I really didn't. Fatigue ran high. Two weeks previously I had put up half my house in a 15 by 10 storage unit in Flower Mound, Texas. My house up in Denton was not selling and I was not even sure if I chose the right part of town to live in Shanghai.

But this was how Mone and I first made contact. It was most definitely not the warmest first introductions.

In my brain, I know I was to be an aroma of Christ. But just two weeks into a new city, I found it hard to play gracious visitor. Our front doors were side by side. So I told her we would try.

She smiled, happy that I complied. 谢谢. "Thank you," she acknowledged and closed her door.

The next day, she sent over two plates of homemade dumplings. She told me her mother made it. The one with the heart problems? I remember the words of wisdom: "When in Rome, do what the Romans do."

So I became Shanghainese. I sent over a small sample of my beef bourguignon. Her husband, a stately sort of a man in the quarry business, opened the door and thanked me politely.

"That woman is crazy, Ma!" I tell my mom on the phone over long distance. She came over and oiled my door! Right there, for 20 minutes! Repeating it twice so that my mother could hear me loud and clear.

Mom had met her and I was so sure she would agree with my justified rants. She listened, and instead of agreeing, simply said, "她是没事的" (She is alright.) With that, she moved on to give me tips on how to buy food cheaply from the locals.

Jesus! Surely, I am not sent thousands of miles across the ocean to have "awful" neighbors? But when the Bible said, "The Lord will watch over your coming and going both now and forevermore" (Psalm 128:1), God meant it.

One day, I heard a strange noise. Something out of the ordinary. I listened closer. My heart skipped a beat. Could it be? Yes, it was! It was the sound of a cello!

This went on for a while. Every now and then, we heard cello sounds coming from our neighbor's apartment. Our boys on the other hand, practiced at closing our front door gently. "Softer a bit," she would still sometimes say. "So sorry!" I would duly say.

151

If it is possible, as far as it depends on you, live at peace with everyone. Romans 12:18

Make every effort to live in peace with everyone and to be holy; without holiness no one will see the Lord. See to it that no one falls short of the grace of God and that no bitter root grows up to cause trouble and defile many. Hebrews 12:14-15

Many times, it was not easy to keep peace with all around us. It was hard enough already at home, especially when everyone had a rough day. Thankfully, our boisterous boys did finally learn. Frank, our neighbor's 15 year old son, also did get better at his cello. We learned to live peaceably with one another living in close quarters.

Later on, I discovered in passing conversation that Mone was a Christian. I was delighted to find this out. We had lunch together one time, and she shared with me how she came to faith and then it all clicked. All those questions about marriage arose because she is the only Christian in her family. I guess she was watching us. Maybe that is why God placed us as neighbors.

"Can you help?" Mone asked me one day. Her son wanted to go to an English school here and needed some conversational practice for the school interview.

"I can find you a British tutor," I volunteered, "He has a TON of teaching credentials."

"No, we want you. If your husband can help as well, it would even be better," she said.

"Do you like 菜饭 (cai fan)? I'll have my mom make you some. It is an oily Shanghainese dish," she explained.

I am not sure I like an oily food as a gift, but I thanked her politely nonetheless. We wrestled for a moment if we wanted to be that engaged in their lives. After all, Ron kept late working hours in Shanghai and every night, we found ourselves busy helping the boys with their Chinese homework. In other words, we were swimming with quite a load ourselves. But there was no end to all that work and since we knew it was an opportunity to be of service, we said "yes".

We looked over the interview questions she sent us. We studied Frank's essay. The Spirit was at work in us and stirred us into willing service. Frank would come over, sometimes in his pajamas, and practiced his English with us. Some nights, the boys also took turns practicing English with him and it proved to be a fun exercise of role reversals for them.

Soon, we found ourselves rooting for her son to win. We asked Frank about his dreams. (He wants to start a company.) And where he was headed. (Stanford..in the US). This was a kid obviously wanting to go places. His grandmother roots for him. His parents work hard and also root for him. We were just happy to play a small part in his life.

We gave him a Jesus placue ("Footprints") as a gift of encouragement. We took time to pray with him. After a couple of these practice interviews, I figured it was time to relax. So going out on a limb, I asked if he would play the cello for us.

153

He took our request seriously and played us a difficult piece. His mother stood close by, flipping the page whenever one page was done. Our family sat captured, in the small living room, listening to the music played by this fine young man. So this is how Yo Yo Ma and Casals did it: sheer practice, backed by loving support and commitment from others.

Finally when we heard news that he was accepted into the American school, we gave him a leather bound Bible. "Remember God as you pursue your dreams," we encouraged him.

The day when we left for the US, I knocked on Mone's door. There was no point carting a fragile piece of glass vase home. So I gave her my Jurlique-styled vase with two symbolic bamboo stems in them. "They represent our sons," I said. "Please enjoy them."

Two months later, I emailed her to say hello. She responded warmly and attached a picture. "See how your 'sons' are growing!"

When we open the Bible, we notice a story like the Good Samaritan. In His good wisdom, God seems to share this story as if to make a plea with us. Let the differences dissolve away, He seems to say. Yes, you all are different but you who belong to me -- show mercy.

We started as two women thrown together first by close proximity as neighbors. We both did things that annoyed the other. Over time and with God's love, we found as sisters in Christ we had some kind of common mission in life.

Section 5 – Proclaiming the Cross

"I speak the truth in Christ." Romans 9:1

/Angela/ "耶稣爱你！ Jesus loves you!" says Betty. She is my four year old friend, and a friend to everyone at the Starbucks near us. The baristas find her cute. Maybe that is my cue. From the mouth of babes…a four year old with no fear. It is not the powerful or the super-rich or the super-privileged I write about. Their stories are covered and followed already.

In China, at least in the Shanghai I know, the lame are here. So are the blind on the subways. And yes, definitely the poor at the foot of overhead pedestrian bridges. And of course the beggars at the tourist spots and outside the church entrance. There are the millions who take the metro (subway) every day, the office workers, the teachers, the shopkeepers, the street sweepers, the entrepreneurs and expatriates--they are all here.

Some have heard the message, many more have not. There are too few Betty's around, fearless four year olds who speak the simple truth.

[Chapter 41] 20 Exits and More

"For you created my inmost being; you knit me together in my mother's womb.   I praise you because I am fearfully and wonderfully made; your works are wonderful, I know that full well. My frame was not hidden from you when I was made in the secret place. When I was woven together in the depths of the earth, your eyes saw my unformed body. All the days ordained for me were written in your book before one of them came to be." Psalm 139:13-16.

/Angela/   Sometimes when I do not feel like exploring outside, I would get off the train at People's Square station.   The endless waves of commuters streaming from one exit to another never fails to amaze me.

The sea of faces change every few minutes each time the trains drop off a fresh supply of commuters. The sight of constant motion, an ocean of thousands of people moving from one place to another, is mesmerizing to watch.

Everyone except the few out-of-towners seems to know exactly where to go next, how to move with the crowd.

After several months here, I am at home in Shanghai now. I have a similar face, being Chinese myself. But because my roots are foreign, I feel out of place no matter how adept I have become at living here.

I am determined to make the most of my time here and not squander it. At the People's Square (人民广场) station in the center of Shanghai's metro system, even with endless waves of people, there is a certain orderliness in the human traffic flow. There are 20 exits around the People's Square station. I finally figure out that if I head over to Exit 3, I can find well priced Apple accessories sold by a brother and sister from Fujian province.

I didn't really come here for the shopping, though. I came to watch the people, all 700,000 of this massive group that will pass through this station today. This endless throng of people, each person God says is important, and it makes me take a second look and try to see more.

I see the office worker, all prim and proper, looking confident, knowing full well his next stop. Head buried in his smartphone, thumb scrolling the screen fast and intentional. I see the confused peasant family from the province, oblivious to city etiquette. They do not look for the bathroom. Instead, they have their child pee on the subway platform. I see the old folks. They are warmly dressed in their puffy winter clothes, going about the city they've witnessed much change in. I also see a great number of migrant workers, clearly identified by their calloused hands and heavy sun-tanned faces.

Many young people from all over China are found here too, not so suave-looking like the local Shanghainese. They are lured to the city by the idea of better job prospects and following the latest trends here.

There is something about being a foreigner. Things people take for granted, we see with different eyes and minds. This massive human sea. Such a huge crowd at one spot. It makes me curious, wanting to know the stories behind these people.

Where are they going? When they finally arrive at their destination, will they be happy or frustrated?

It is a question we need to ask ourselves about our lives. It applies not just for commuters in the subways. If God says we are all precious in His sight, what does it really mean about how we ought to live our lives? Do we look up and ask only when we see our destination coming?

In my second year in Shanghai, a young American friend traveling in China with her mom informed me of a new app that young people in the US were using called "Snapchat." It allows its users to take photos, record videos, add text and drawings, and send them to a controlled list of recipients. The photographs and videos sent were known as "Snaps" and the idea was it allowed users to post anything they like because they disappear soon after being opened because of the time limit set. Once they are gone, they are really gone and not recoverable.

In God's eyes, we are not just snaps, even though it feels like it sometimes. We are not living throwaway lives with a long succession of deleted moments. Each minute matters. With so many of us on this blue planet, how could we each possibly be *that* important to Him? But we are.

[Chapter 42] The Power of One

/Angela/ I met Diana on a Saturday night service at an international church outreach called Grace Extended. She sat on my left side while the rest of my family took their seats on my right. Toward the end of the service. I turned toward her, said hello and then asked if she was in a small group. She said "no" and we invited her to ours.

Months later we had a chance to meet her mom who was visiting in town. Diana's mother, a youthful looking woman, told us that she literally lived next door to the church building growing up in Taiwan. "There really was no escaping!" Diana's mother quipped.

The result? Everyone in her family received Christian influence as a consequence. This journey of faith started with Diana's grandmother--only one woman—and her decision to dedicate her life and family to Christ. This woman is an old lady I have not met and she is God's faithful servant.

This is how the story went. There was war. Food was scarce. Many Christian missionaries came and gave the country light and hope. The grandmother was one of the many that rece ved such unconditional goodness. Grateful, she vowed like Hannah in the Bible, and gave herself and her family to Christ.

Of course, not all followed in faithfulness. One of those children was Diana's mother. Baptized over 50 years ago, she was quick to acmit her rebellious ways in earlier years. Now older and wiser, she carries with her a spirit of God's grace.

We had all gathered at their home in Shanghai listening to their faith story before a delicious spread of food by prepared by the Shanghainese housekeeper. Diana's mother was so proud of her baptismal certificate that she left the table and went looking for it in her purse. It made me wonder where mine went. A simple paper testifying to an earlier decision but one that is able to breathe new life if a person takes the call seriously.

Our small family home group met every other week. We tried to keep it simple: prayer time, perhaps a song or two, time spent studying the Word together. Here is one of our meeting notes sent out by email.

(Email Invite by Diana .... Lesson notes and questions by Ron)

When a person knows they are about to leave this world and they have a chance to speak to those they leave behind, we get a chance to see what they really value, what they believe and what's important. We turn to John 13, the beginning of a section (John 13-17) that captures Jesus' last words to his disciples. Listen to what Jesus says and notice especially what he does.

Read John 13 and take a moment to look ahead to what is in chapters 14-17 as well.

1. In John 1-12 how has Jesus already shown his disciples that he loved them?

2. Is there any connection between verse 3 and verses 4-5? What does Jesus know, and how does that affect his actions?

3. What example has Jesus set for you to follow (vv. 13-15)? Have you seen any way recently to apply this to your life?

160

4. What according to Jesus secures God's blessing (v. 17)?

5. Judas betrays Jesus. Peter later denied Jesus. What were they missing?

6. What is the distinctive mark of being Jesus' follower according to him (vv. 34-35)? Are you growing in this?

Challenging questions, and a very challenging passage from John 13. Come this Friday and expect to be blessed!

Dinner is included. If you plan to invite new friends, welcome and let me know!

We were covering John 13-17 that Friday at our small group. Our hearts were heavy about our announced departure from China. We now understand what it feels like to leave behind young friends mid-journey. There were times at the beginning where we felt bewildered at our calling but gatherings like this help us remember that the Lord is in control.

I am especially thankful to have met Diana. She continued in her faith, first grabbed on by her grandmother and then passed on to her mother, who in turn passed it on to her. Diana started a Bible group study when she was in Harvard Business School and then made sure she continued a Christian lifeline in Boston. In Shanghai, in spite of crazy work schedules, she remembered how much fellowship in the Christian ring was useful. And that was how we met and connected.

Her fellow alumni friends joined. Our local church also sent us contacts who were interested in a small group in the city. The other day I received a happy email that one of them who came to our group as a seeker was baptized in San Francisco. The circle of Christian friends grows wider, bigger and deeper.

China continues to grow, even if the feverish pace has slowed a bit. All over the country, buildings go up through the efforts of many. The movement of Christ and the advancement of His Kingdom on the other hand often starts small. I have seen it many times over in China and elsewhere.

It really is quite simple: One obedient heart equals many lives changed.

Will you be that one, even if the results are not clearly seen immediately?

[Chapter 43] Sharing at Frank's

/Angela/ "So, what kind of a Christian are you?" Frank finally asked me one day.

He sat himself across our table while the kids ate his delicious Taiwanese noodles and Ron and I had his homemade "set lunches" (daily specials).

We had been going to his cafe for a while now. To him and us, we were his 老顾客("old customers")。Frank had gotten to adopt us somehow.

Sometimes when the crowd thinned out after the Saturday lunch, he would revel the kids with stories of snakes that hide up in the bamboo found only in Taiwan. The boys thought it was cool these snakes could camouflage themselves so well. But I made a mental note to not visit such danger-filled places.

His shop is tucked away in a small alley off one of the main artery roads in Lujiazui.   There are fancier looking places that draw the office crowd but Frank cooks without MSG. And most of all, he puts his heart into his food daily.

The name of his shop in Chinese still escapes me. In our family we call it "Frank's". After that, all the friends we bring to his cafe call it "Frank's" too.

"Huh?" I go.   It's my usual response of incomprehension. I'm back to Frank's question about the flavor of my Christian belief.

"You know, there are many kinds of Christians and denominations," Frank said.

"Oh," I go in my head. This is my opening. I ought to know how to respond. I am trying to recall the 4 steps of belief or the 5 distinctives of faith that I have been taught. The acronyms eloquently taught to me hundreds of times in sermons and Bible classes go *completely* blank in me.

So, I summon what I think captures it best.

I reply, "I am the kind who follows Jesus. 我是跟耶稣的."

He looks at me through his bespectacled face. He gets it. This man who has seen the world, made his pile, read and studied much.

When I first came to Shanghai, I thought I had my stuff together. I could make a case for Christ. But China has taught me something. Hang around a while, live with the people, do your chores, buy your groceries, eat your food. Sometimes very soon or other times much later, they do get curious and eventually they do ask.

"So, what kind of Christian are you?"

Hopefully, all the days of my life, I can just simply say, " I am the kind who follows Jesus."

[Chapter 44] An Unlikely Friend

/Angela/ "So where are you from?" Shi Ayi asked me, a complete fish out of water. She was seated among a group of gray-headed Shanghainese. She obviously knew who she was, where *she* came from.

She was seated on a stool, her face half twisted with a smirk, almost sure I couldn't answer. The answer, you see, wasn't where I just came from. It would have been simple to rattle off the answer, "America" or "I was born in Singapore". That would have been an easy answer.

What Shi Ayi wanted to know was, as all nuances go in any language, do I know my roots, did I understand the trees and rivers that fed my fathers five generations ago?

"Huizhou", I shot back quickly, still unsure of my lineage many times. (But that is another story.) The stare down game ended almost abruptly. She relaxed. I went "whew" in my head. I had established and won genuine admiration.

Shi Ayi was a Godsend. How we ended up as friends from such a face-off encounter still baffles me today. But I did know right from the beginning that our meeting was a divinely appointed one.

In a shop at the wet market where locals mingled for friendly chats and gossip, we met. I happened to be there one midmorning, seeking help for a pinched nerve. Too overwhelmed to tackle their behemoth medical system, I decided to do what my mother recommended. In simple advice: Ask the locals. Talk to people. In other words, don't google, wiki and be anti-social. So, off I went and did just that.

We soon became friends after that short detente. I found out she divorced in the seventies, in an era where the whole country was diligent to 扫盲. It meant "sweep away blindness" literally. It was a radical and intense movement led by the Communist government that was to stamp out not only illiteracy, but rid blindness of every kind. The idea of walking out on her husband, raising her son on her own, in a time when "Little House on the Prairie" was familiar American family fare on TV just blew my mind away.

Shi Ayi taught me culture, Chinese words and most importantly the gumption that gave me the ability and confidence to communicate further and better with other Shanghainese during my time there. On the other hand, I was relentless in sharing the message of Christ with her.

"Oh, Christ!" she said with some excitement, "I have heard of him."

"In fact, when I was a little girl, my grandmother would say prayers during the mealtimes!" she exclaimed. I looked at this woman, slightly older than my mother and realized that we were really not any different in soul and spirit. We all hear things, we all see things, but what gets awakened and pursued, that really depends on us and our willingness to hear and see.

Sometime last year, she went to Hunan. "What for?" I asked as I scanned the map of China to locate it. "To help my son's girlfriend's mom's business," she replied.

"You are doing what?!?" I remember asking, voice half rising. Then I remember, everything coming back to me, all my understanding about Chinese culture.

For Shi Ayi, her entire life had been to do her best and give it all to raise her son. This girlfriend he had was not a relationship that she approved of but what was there to do or say? Adult children have their own minds and wills. Problems with her grown son was not something I could offer much help in. After all, mine are only 8 and 10 years old. Teach her to pray, perhaps? Maybe the stinging emotion of "upset" would dissolve and leave.

I encouraged her to talk to God, and this is what I heard: "Dear God, I really want the relationship to end. Please stop it for me. I do not want my son to be with her anymore."

It wasn't the kind of prayer I was expecting but I didn't want Shi Ayi to just sit there and watch me pray for her either. I told her we could pray about the situation but really inside, I have no clue what to pray. When she said what she did, I realized maybe the best answers come from turning to the Bible. So we did.

"If any of you lacks wisdom, you should ask God, who gives generously to all without finding fault, and it will be given to you." James 1:5

"Let us turn to the Bible," I said. Dutifully, she did. I had been diving into the Bible a lot more lately, so this was no longer just another book in the house but something I could use to help another life traveler. When Shi Ayi complied, I knew then that our relationship was no longer where it was when it started over a year ago. What might have been a fleeting acquaintance

167

became an opportunity for us to draw closer to God and to one another.

Shi Ayi's prayer reminded me that as sinners, our hearts are indeed clouded. We want what we think is good for us. But Lord, what do you want? None hits closer to home than a simple question posed by my friend.

Janet said, "I know what you want." (To sell our house in the US.) "But is this what the Lord wants?" Ron and I took pause. She is right. Lord, what do you want?

You know what I want. But Lord, Giver of Life, Ruler of all Things, what do you want?

Asking that question is hard. Because quite honestly, I may not like the answer. Or follow it, for that matter. I called Shi Ayi today, a few weeks after my trip to Singapore. She told me her son was getting married in September and she was on her way to Gansu (another place I needed to look up on the map) to fix up a property for him. I reminded her to pray. I felt her nod over the phone. Silently I prayed she would read the Bible I gave her and not let God belong to her grandmother only but become living for her as well.

" .. for your Father knows what you need before you ask him." Matthew 6:6-8

A month ago, Shi Ayi tracked me down and we were able to reunite again. Her first words after she sat down at my apartment were, "Guess what? They broke up!"

"God heard you!" I said. Wow, He did!

168

Still a little unsure, she said, "8 years! I never thought it possible."

I know. I too, after 25 years as a Christian, still do not believe at times. Does our good God really care? Does He really hear? And when I get what I want, does that mean He is real and good? When I am in the midst of difficult waiting and He seems silent, does that mean He doesn't exist and is no longer true?

I have to learn that in all that is difficult and crazy, God is still good. Establish that God is good.

Yes, establish that our God is good.

[Chapter 45] Fellowship

"They were staying in the apostles' teaching and with the fellowship, continuing to break bread and persisting in prayer" Acts 2:42 (my translation)

\Ron\ When you move to a new place, it can take a while to feel settled in. I have moved many times in my life, and one of the difficulties of moving for me is making new friends. Belonging to a local church is one of the ways to quickly get plugged in.

I can still recall the amazement of one of Angela's long-time friends when we moved to Shanghai and within our first few weeks we mentioned that we were attending a local church. "So fast?" the friend asked, finding it hard to believe the speed with which we found a local community of faith.

For some people, church is a place of ritual or routine, or a place you go to in search of divine favor. For our family, it has usually been about fellowship.

In one of the movies based on Tolkien's books, The Fellowship of the Ring, an unlikely collection of very different individuals is brought together for a common goal, accompanying the hobbit Frodo Baggins on a perilous journey. Some of the members of the group are wary and untrusting of others. The unity of the group is threatened more than once. But that idea of sharing something in common even in the face of great differences is what makes them a fellowship.

The Chinese have a similar ancient story that is well-known and beloved in their culture called Journey to the West. A small band of very different characters are also on a long journey that is beset by difficulties but also filled with adventures. The result is the same: a strong bond of fellowship is formed by these varied travelers.

I did not quickly form a kinship or fellowship with many of the Chinese I met in China. I made efforts to understand the culture, the shared experiences that made people think and act the way they did. I was still surprised to discover that our attitudes and interpretations of those same events and people were often quite different. Over time, I slowly did come to understand better.

I experienced fellowship with a man who had moved to China at almost the same time we did and who was from the same city in the US. We didn't live close to each other in Shanghai or see each other often, but when we got together there was a deep sense that we were going through the same kind of experience together.

At one point we got to sit together at a two-day leadership conference. There were times of small group sharing and discussion as a part of this conference, and that naturally fed into a stronger bond and understanding between us.

That conference was a telecast of the Global Leadership Summit that Bill Hybels and the Willow Creek Community Church in Barrington, Illinois, organize every year. One of Bill's famous quotes is, "The local church is the hope of the world," and he believes that fervently. He has put his life's work into building up a strong local church that truly has a global impact and equipping others to build community and fellowship that is focused on Christ.

I know there are people who have not had a positive church experience or who were even hurt or damaged at a church instead of nurtured in fellowship. We were even part of a church once that attracted a large number of people from such backgrounds and provided a healing place for them. Jesus certainly knew and even warned about religious people like the Pharisees who would be more of an obstacle than a help to those seeking God.

Several years into his public ministry as Jesus was on a wave of popularity, he was welcomed into Jerusalem by enthusiastic crowds and followers. He wanted to celebrate the Passover with his closest disciples and as they broke bread together, he dropped a bombshell on them: one of them would betray him.

Betrayal! It's the opposite of fellowship, a close relationship reversed, corrupted, broken. This very group, deprived of their leader, reduced in number by Judas' suicide, compromised by Peter's denial, racked by doubts like Thomas', had to find a way forward. We also have to choose whether we will hold on to hurt or seek healing.

Early in the book of Acts after Jesus departs earth we are told the disciples gathered their remnants together and remained constant in prayer (Acts 1:14). Out of this, they started to rebuild the community, replacing Judas, renewing their commitment and waiting on God.

The cross brought them together rather than leaving them fractured, and the Spirit of God gave them unity and power. They were soon joined by thousands more, and in every possible way they grew closer together. Absorbing and applying the teachings of Jesus recounted through the apostles, spending time together and sharing meals remembering Jesus, and constantly praying—this is how they build fellowship (Acts 2:42).

In Shanghai, our family started from the beginning to plug into Abundant Grace International Fellowship (AGIF). In more recent years, foreigners in China have gradually been given more freedom to meet together and worship and form communities of faith. AGIF had several hundred members from six continents, many countries and different languages and very diverse Christian backgrounds come together for an English fellowship.

It was not an unusual occurrence to find people who grew much closer to God and more vital in their faith during their time in Shanghai. Whether they came from the UK, South Africa, Venezuela, Iran, the US, France, Tanzania, the Netherlands or Ghana, their time in China unexpectedly challenged them and brought them closer to the fellowship of the cross.

We were particularly drawn to an outreach of AGIF called Grace Extended which intentionally welcomed the younger people and those who were seeking something other than the traditional church environment. There was a freedom and energy in those gatherings, an exuberance that came from praying fervently and worshipping gladly and pursuing God with heart-felt hunger and thirst.

Of course it doesn't just happen on its own. We have to take a step, to put ourselves in the middle of a collision course with fellow travelers. This happened to us in several ways. One was through a small group that met in our home every few weeks. We opened up our home and let God send our way those who were willing. Another was through a trip to the Chinese countryside.

On that trip we grew closer to another family with young kids who were attending our church. Like us, their time in Shanghai was transformative and kindled a deeper faith.

We also grew closer to the Chinese people themselves, identifying with what we have in common rather than what makes us different. The generosity and sharing of people richer than us in graciousness and hospitality and gratitude was humbling.

One other experience of deeper fellowship came when AGIF decided to get away from the city for a weekend and to spend time in worship and teaching and sharing. We called it a retreat, not in the sense of falling back from the battle line but as a way to get away from the buzz and frenzy of the city (Shanghai has over 20 million people in it) and to focus our time on seeking God and forming stronger bonds as fellow believers.

The cross gives us a common focal point in our life journey. Let's face it: it's easy to get distracted or diverted from truly important things in our modern lifestyle. The cultures we live in, awash in information and entertainment, media and mobile devices, often have us running around and yet unfulfilled, temporarily absorbed, yet bored with life.

What happens if you unplug, start having real and vital human conversations with real people that are not like you in any obvious ways? Can you imagine that? If you can at least imagine it, could you go through with living in *that* reality and not escape to your virtual reality mediated through technology? I challenge you to do just that. Take a 30 day entertainment and technology fast.

Don't just abstain, though. Replace the absence of technology with a pouring in of real fellowship, no matter how unlikely. What do you need to give up? Who will you engage in real conversation? Who is someone you can bless with a coat, a blanket, a drink or a word of encouragement? When you do this, you are one step closer to true fellowship—a common purpose united around something true that is bigger than you imagine.

[Chapter 46] We Are a New Family

/Angela/ The other day, I met a 保姆 (nanny) a few blocks from our apartment by the Huangpu River. She saw me reading. I had my Bible and journal with me.

"Are you a Christian?" she asked.

"Yes."

"Me too," she beamed.

She whipped up her Bible verses on a sticky note and started reading it. She had a simple, country folk kind of look and yet the Spirit of Grace was living sweetly in her.

"I do not know English," she told me. "But I just knew you must be reading the Bible. I am so glad to meet you," she said.

I found myself having to drop my need to be left alone. That morning, I was searching for what God had to say to me in Psalms. I was not convinced that He would respond. I read His Word but the words there did not come alive. Knowing how hard I was searching, He sent a living answer instead.

She told me about the family she was serving. Two doctors, three adopted Chinese kids. One of the kids was going to be sent to the US for more surgeries.

"Lots of complications," she said. I understood. Many adopted Chinese babies need surgeries.

"God is good," I offered.

"Yes," she agreed. We paused for a minute and looked at the two babies she was caring for in their strollers. Our minds wandered in our own spaces. I did not know these people but my heart was woken to gratitude for their Albert Schweitzer hearts.

There was a lot of things unsaid that morning but that is what going to the riversice to listen to God does. Amid the din in the city, it invites a pause if you let it. I thought of the verse in John 15:5 where Jesus says, "I am the vine; you are the branches." He is right. When we abide in Him, we bear much fruit and one that doesn't bear fruit has no use. It is thrown into the fire and burned. (John 15:6)

Being a nanny isn't a glamorous job. But for these two infants, it is a gift of a new life. Because of her contribution, these young lives are not abandoned or brought up with too little love in an orphanage or sold as sex slaves without any clue that their lives matter. Because of these doctors who adopted them, they now carry both an opportunity and responsibility to pass on that goodness when they are grown up. Christ does change lives. I see it often in the many families that adopt the Chinese kids at our church here.

We are different, it is clear," she said and then she continued, "But Christ's Spirit binds us all together. How wonderful."

It is the same words a woman slightly younger than my mother's age uttered to me when I was on our Anhui mission trip. The Chinese women on that bus wanted to know my story, how I came to be at their village, why I chose to come to China and what did I learn from the world out there.

My blood runs Chinese. I am two generations removed from this soil but I still "get" them, and they get me. Will I really connect with people if I am in Africa or India, the remotest places for me? I didn't think I could but I am beginning to see that perhaps I can too.

And why? Because Christ binds us together. Just like what the nanny said. By Christ's blood and our desire to carry the Cross, we become a new family.

[Chapter 47] Time with My Florist

/Angela/ This past Spring, I noticed a new floral shop on my street after the crosswalk. It was a few doors away from the Sex Toys shop with its bold sign and it breathed like fresh air into the space of a former liquor and cigarette store, also a shop I disliked tremendously.

I popped into the shop one day and what a treat it was! It turned out that the owner of the shop was a Christian woman.   Ka Mi had such a pleasant countenance about her that I felt inspired to buy flowers for people from her. The name of her shop? "Heaven Sent Floral Designs".

From the get go, it was her spirit that won my heart over. The street where her shop fronts was not the most ideal. One would often find trash left outside by the food vendors nearby. Her shop was small and her heavy chain smoking husband preferred taking orders from her. It would be hard on a woman's soul to thrive under such circumstances but God's grace filled the gaps of a broken heart here.

In Ka Mi's case, come what may, she faithfully does the work God assigned her. Each day, she tends her shop, listens closely to what her customers want, raises her almost grown son now and makes beautiful floral arrangements. No request, whether it is small or big, escapes without loving attention from her. Except when she is not around, that is.

"Other people may not notice it," she spoke out loud as I watched in rapt attention the details she put into my limited budget floral purchase.

"But I do and the Lord does," she continued as she put the final touches to her work for me.

"Do your best to present yourself to God as one approved, a worker who does not need to be ashamed and who correctly handles the word of truth." 2 Timothy 2:15

"So, what do you say? Do you think Jesus is already here?" Ka Mi asked the other day. And herein lies the remarkable quality of our "business" relationship. Each time I popped in, there was business to do but we often found time to encourage one another in our faith.

"I met a friend the other day," she plunged right in after I made known my request. "She is a fervent believer and she informs me that Jesus is in China this moment and there is another book I need to read to be prepared. What do you say?"

I am no preacher, pastor or minister but China does not have a church on every street corner or many teachers deeply grounded in sound bible teaching either. I gave up the conversation in my head that I have no good answers.

So instead I said, "What did you tell her?" I genuinely wanted to know.

"I told her that the Bible is enough, " she responded back as she gingerly placed one flower on top of another. "It is God breathed and all that I need to know is there."

Her resolution was clear but even more clearly, the unmistakable spirit of Grace filled the answer. There was no put down at all.

"What do you say?" Ka Mi asked. She was asking me not because she didn't know the answer. She asked because she knew as fellow Christians, we all could sharpen one another.

"As iron sharpens iron, one person sharpens another." Proverbs 27:17.

What does God say? And that is what we are to be for one another as sisters in Christ.

So I affirm her. "You answered correctly," I said, "God's Word is indeed enough."

She affirms me as well. This bravado to come to China, make a living the local way and put my kids in the China school system. "It is not easy," she said, "But God is with you."

It never occurred to me that Ka Mi and I would enjoy this brief sweet friendship when I first visited her store. In a city where so many things were overpriced, I was delighted to find her. The harshness of the city is not lost on many of us. The human striving for financial swagger is strong and spiritual maturity is barely sought by most.

The soothing balm that Christians bring should not be overlooked. This is what I think sweet fellowship means. I may not know every name or background of every believer but when Christian believers meet, we are one in Spirit and truth. Not jostling for attention and no need to impress. Not finding fault but affirming instead. Just a desire to serve one another.

" ... May they be brought to complete unity to let the world know that you sent me and have loved them even as you loved me." John 17:23

181

[Chapter 48] Family Worship

"A time is coming—in fact, has already arrived—when true worshippers will worship the Father in spirit and truth, for they are the kind of worshippers the Father seeks. God is Spirit, and his worshippers must worship him in spirit and truth." John 4:23-24

\Ron\ Before we went to China we were part of a small group that met every other week to read a book together, pray and encourage each other. We had been part of small groups since the early 90's in Singapore and knew how much we benefitted from these gatherings. Looking back, the times we did not meet with a group were lonely times in our spiritual walk. They were also times with little fruit to show for claims of spiritual growth.

Soon after arriving in Shanghai we decided to host a home meeting in our apartment in downtown. The church we were a part of did not have any regular groups meeting there at the time but were eager to get one started.

Chee Ming was a sincere and selfless elder of the church who agreed to come and join us early on. A senior staff person tried to connect us to others who lived nearby and were interested in a group with a promise to send others who showed interest.

Those first few months we had two other families and several individuals who came somewhat regularly. The single ladies especially embraced our family and we welcomed them.

Although we sent out a Bible reading assignment and some questions before the group met, probably the most significant thing we did was to pray together in

182

those meetings. The apartment complex where we lived was called Summit in English, so this became our Summit Group. After a few months the elder who supported us initially transitioned out graciously and left us to solidify our group.

Some weeks it was trying just to get our boys settled down, the family fed, and then to receive our guests. We didn't know for sure who would show up each time we met, but we made it a point to pray, to open a corner for the light to shine in our new adopted home.

Besides our family group, we also were learning to draw closer to God at church as our times of worship became intimate and sometimes intense experiences of calling out to God, seeking Him and seeking answers to our struggles, our questions, our doubts. The international church we were a part of was an assembly of people from different countries and continents, and different religious backgrounds and traditions.

One thing we missed was regular, weekly communion around the table of the Lord. Our boys had only become believers in the past year before we came to China, and we felt the need to feed our young so they could grow. The family of Christian faith has regularly taken the meal that Jesus started just before he left earth, both to remember Christ and also to draw ongoing faith and sustenance from our living connection to him.

Around the dining table in our apartment we gathered each weekend to remember what Jesus had done and to draw strength from sharing a meal together to remember Him. The meal was starkly simple: bread and grape juice. We each brought our Bibles to the table and invited each person to share a scripture or

183

verse that was meaningful to them. A single verse from the Psalms. An entire chapter from Joshua. Or nothing at all if someone was blank. Prayers could be offered, forgiveness asked or offered as the Spirit led, a word of encouragement shared or a strong challenge given.

The rest of the story is we often had fights and family arguments going on before these meal times. It took all we could summon to get everyone to sit down together at the table when we would rather not, or when the boys wanted to play video games, or someone wanted to exercise or go out to eat, when one or more of us was sulking or sullen or disagreeable.

We came to see that all of this is not unusual and even has a predictable nature to it.   Diversions and distractions *will* arise.   What is necessary is the purposeful cultivation of faith, the regular efforts to get ourselves rooted.   Some competing spiritual force or power did not want us to be united, to focus our attention on Christ and the cross and to draw strength from it.

These were holy moments. This was real worship. By setting this up, we were making a serious proclamation about God and not letting our emotions set the agenda.

As parents we often prayed for and with our boys before they went to bed. We sent them off to school with a blessing or prayer. We gathered in their bedroom, looking out from our fifth floor window across the street and directly into the windows of our sons' classrooms or onto the marching field where students gathered and we prayed for them. "God, make them a light. Let them shine today. God protect them from moral danger and Satan's darts and lies. Help them grow into young men who make a difference in this world."

We included our boys in the home group meetings of the Summit Group. Since these meetings would go for more than an hour, they sometimes found it hard to stay focused or even awake! The winter months were especially hard. Even when we had no guests and the group was only the four of us, we would nevertheless take time to pray and set aside the time and not give up on hosting the home meeting.

In our second year the group started meeting in someone else's apartment and we didn't lead the discussion every week. We were learning to share the duties. This group was a part of our natural rhythm and the boys looked forward to these meetings as much as anyone. "Train up a child in the way they should go..." and they will develop a heart for worship and a desire to serve God. This is an act of faith, and the Lord will reward perseverance.

This was not all for the childrens' sake either. They became our accountability partners and kept us on task. *We* needed this routine, this faith habit as much as they did. Faith grows when it is shared, when we have to really exercise it. It is an act of faith to continue walking the path even when you don't see the fruit and when everything that meets the eyes and assaults the ears seems contrary to the goal to grow faith.

The answer is to die. Return to the cross. Give up your illusions about perfect family devotions, about Bible reading that always gives you inspiration without fail. One foot behind the other, following Christ to the cross. The ecstasy, the agony, the purpose and the sacrifice. It all is for something, of this I am sure.

And I am *assured* that it is not lost on a God who takes notice of every sparrow that needs feeding and every lily growing in the grass and who cares for you and me much more than these birds and flowers. Believe it is so and act on it. This is an act of worship.

[Chapter 49] Tongues

"...with your blood you purchased people for God from every tribe and language and people and nation." Revelation 5:9b

\Ron\ When you uproot and move to a new country and are facing a foreign culture, you look for the comforts of home like a drowning man flails about for a life preserver. A snatch of your own language heard on the street, someone who you recognize, a smile or show of human kindness—these become rare treats.

Why give up the comforts of home to strike out and go somewhere foreign and unknown in the first place? As Christians it is because we sense the call of God. Beyond this there is a side benefit: the strange and unpredictable has its rewards as well as its difficulties.

One of the benefits I gained from learning the original languages of the Bible (Hebrew, Aramaic and Greek) when I was younger is that it forces you to slow down your reading so that you pay closer attention to the words and meaning rather than skimming over what can become too familiar.

It is also rewarding to hear the glories and wonders of God expressed in another tongue and to get another insight into the richness of the gospel. I recall a prayer meeting in a Chinese church in which the believers were passionately beseeching the Lord for the salvation of their families and people they knew and singing praises to God in their own tongue. It was moving, and also a foretaste of heaven to me.

On the other hand, it's not fun to feel on the outside looking in on a conversation. That happened countless times for me. I should know what's going on, and I can guess fairly well, but I'm not quick enough to follow the rapid-fire dialogue, not fluent enough to jump in and make an appropriate comment.

These were "back to the cross" moments which required me to swallow my pride and to acknowledge I'm not as smart or clever as I thought I was. To learn another language truly requires you to become like a child again, making mistakes and being misunderstood and taking the risk that you will make a mess of someone else's mother tongue. Regardless of all that, it is worth the effort.

There was fervent prayer in the first century after Jesus had left earth and his followers were gathered together, doing exactly what he had told them to do: wait. Pray and wait for the promised gift.

One day when his followers gathered together for prayer, a rushing wind came along with the empowering presence of the Holy Spirit. Tongues of fire appeared over their heads and human languages were instantly given them as they spoke the glories of God in languages that could be understood by far-off visitors to Jerusalem.

More than once I envied those early believers for their God-given ability to speak a language they had neither studied, labored over nor made silly mistakes in speaking. Immediate fluency—how nice that would be!

The miraculous also allows us to see the ordinary and every day in a new light. Many more times since Pentecost God has enabled believers to learn a foreign tongue the *slow* way, the incarnational way, becoming flesh and growing to maturity just as Jesus did when he came to earth.

Jesus learned the languages of Aramaic, Greek and Hebrew as a child and young boy, studying and growing in knowledge over time rather than miraculously all-at-once being given the gift of utterance in these languages. Aramaic was spoken among the common Jewish people and especially in Galilee. Greek was spoken in Egypt, the place Jesus' family fled to soon after his birth. It was also the common tongue of the marketplace, especially in the cities of Judea and Palestine which were already Hellenized. Hebrew was the language of the synagogue which the rabbis taught young Jewish boys as part of their formal education in the Torah (law).

The task of language learning has been repeated many times since the first century by those who carried the good news across cultural and linguistic boundaries to others who have not heard. Whether the gospel has gone to Asia, Europe, Africa or the Americas, it has crossed these borders.

Linguistically speaking, in China there is a standard spoken form of Chinese that can be understood by many people across the country. Standard Chinese (Mandarin) has the most number of speakers in the world. However, there are many local Chinese languages that have traditionally been called dialects. The truth is that most of these are different enough to be considered separate spoken languages because people speaking different local dialects cannot understand each other.

There are also non-Chinese languages within China because there are at least 56 different ethnic groups and in actuality there are more. There are around 300 different languages in China alone.

When I traveled from Shanghai to other places like Zhejiang, Guangzhou, Guangxi and Yunnan, I met people who were educated in Chinese and who could speak it, but their primary spoken language was either a dialect or some other tribal language.

I recall a dinner conversation with a large group in Shenzhen (bordering Hong Kong) in which I asked the question, "What is the most difficult language to learn?" As an American I was thinking of all the languages of the world, European, African, Native American, etc. For this group of Chinese, their first question said a lot: "Domestic or foreign languages?" Given the 300+ languages spoken in China and the almost limitless dialects and local varieties, I saw that the Chinese have their hands full considering a large catalogue of languages without even having to think about the world outside of China.

God of course thinks about the world—the whole world—and so he desires to have the good news proclaimed in every language, every tongue.

What that means, in specific terms, is more than just Bible translation. To have the Scriptures available in a language is just a first step. The good news must be preached, lived out and put into flesh by real people however flawed they may be.

This is one of the scandals of the cross. It is proclaimed by human (which means imperfect) messengers using human (and again imperfect) words. However, God works through these human imperfections by his Holy Spirit to plant and grow faith in the hearts of hearers.

It all starts when a Christ follower is willing to go back to the cross and to share the simple but convicting message of the cross in a way that can be understood and grasped by another person. Are you willing to be the next one to share?

[Chapter 50] Finding God Everywhere: In the City, In the Village

/Angela/ 我会祈祷。("I will pray.")

Her parting words to me as she smiles her dimpled face and bids me goodbye. I watch her go. Her physical transformation in the workplace is remarkable in the short time I know her.

I am not exactly sure why the meeting is necessary. But the prompting to meet her was strong and so I did.

It's been several months since I last saw her. No more frumpy, tentative look. A more confident and prettier self has emerged over a short period of time. Shanghai's work culture has a way of maturing young people fast. In a very brief time, they do the work and take over the workload of three adults over forty years of age in a developed country. That pride is evident in the way they carry themselves.

But behind that polished facade, there is still a person. A soul still trying to find their way and their place in the world. You notice it in the way they fill the silence with questions or chatter. How they twirl their hair or food when they share something deeply personal. Or how they look at you, totally undistracted for a moment, because they truly want to hear the Voice through you, above all their noise inside and around.

That is when you realize that is what you can offer. Not just expensive clothes or gifts but your love, your caring, the opportunity to be Jesus in the flesh with them. Such is the hunger about the dynamic young people of Shanghai. Or maybe everywhere around us too. Just someone to care for them without any agenda.

Who do you turn to when you have parents who fight? How do you find the right wife? What can I do to get ahead? How do I maintain my marriage as the god of work demands my time and seems to demand everything I've got?

If you do not see that their heart cry is the very one you already have experienced, you might just go away not noticing that many of them hurt and some do not even know it.

And pain certainly needs no decoding. You do not even need to know Chinese to get pain.

In the city, in the suburbs and even in small towns, the world tells us that work is a safe refuge to go to. Meaningful work does help, just as rich relationships do. But what happens when that world falls apart? When things do not seem to go the way we like?

Eugene Peterson accurately describes cities as "noisy with self-assertion, forgetful and defiant of God, battering and abusive to persons... What living in cities is good for is making money, acquiring power, practicing deceit." (*Reversed Thunder,* pp. 174,175) But the city is not abandoned in a flight to the countryside leaving it in the hands of hostile forces.

Is God in the city? He sure is. And He has so many of us, His people, in the city. In the suburbs and in the small towns too. And it is cur privilege to be bearers and messengers of the Good News, of a God who still hears, cares and acts. Without a doubt, we truly are "His letters from Christ", "known and read by everybody", "written not with ink but with the Spirit of the Living God" (2 Corinthians 3:2-3)

But with bills to pay, kids half listening, are we really qualified? With no status or power but with our excuses ("that guy is more with it, they have more resources, or the woman is more confident and seasoned, surely not I?") That is where we need prayers. Lots of them. Lord, remove our unbeliefs. Hear our plea.

Now change the scene...

The local Christian at this village where GPS cannot map, tries to explain what is going on. Still, I am refusing to believe. My cognitive mind runs on. They still believe in this stuff? The logic in my head takes the lead in me.

But the group that has gathered on the creaky wooden church bench is united in sincerity. I watch them, their backs facing me as they kneel in prayer for a boy no older than 11 years old.

"He has been sick all his life," a local tells me.

Great pause. The inference being, the whole village knows about his condition.

"As their last resort, they are bringing him to church for healing and prayers," she says.

I have just arrived from the city into a dirt-paved village in China. All around me is strange yet somehow familiar. I have seen pictures of people in the countryside. Not just from pretty National Geographic magazines but from real living family photos.

The people wait in earnest. These are simple farmers who know Psalm 121 not only by heart but they also see it at work. In the yellow-cloaked fields of rapeseed plants they toil, using simple tools, rough machines and a lot of hardworking hands and faith. It is a simple life, an organic pace that runs through the countryside across China.

It is a misnomer to call the church here, in the middle of nowhere, a village church. It defies all my assumptions of what makes a village church. It isn't small. Neither is it dying.

Some five hundred attended the service that morning. I am not sure where all the people had come from or how they did it but they came. They came toward the unfinished massive two story building (they resume construction only when they have the money to do so) in great numbers. And they worshipped the one True God, with attentive ears and heartfelt song.

I am not sure if the praying for the boy brought immediate relief. No "*Talitha koum*" (Mark 5:41) moment here. The boy looks unresponsive still, in stupor. I lean forward and look closer. Amid the anxiety on the adults' faces, the boy looks serenely calm. Perhaps he is the gift?

Oh Lord, help us see. Remove all our unbeliefs!

The believers at hand are not ready to give up. "We will pray some more," they tell each other in Chinese. Within faint earshot, I hear their conversation when they would do that next. Their relentlessness jolts me to a higher reality. Unbelief wants to trail me like a foxhound. But the hounds know they are losing.

Everywhere I go, no matter where I am God seems to want to speak to me. He is waiting. Waiting for me to tune myself to Him and not the noise or distractions in my head. Waiting for me to notice He really is turning ashes into beauty.

He wants my heart. He wants my mind. He wants my soul. He is a jealous God who accepts nothing but all of me. What exactly will I have left if I give even more of me to Him? I do not know but I intend to find out.

Does the Maker of Heaven and Earth care if I ever find a mate? Will my current mate ever be the one I desire him to be? Will my kids turn out alright? Do others really need me? Does God really need me?

Yes, he does.

So we share. We remind ourselves in the work we take on, in the paths we take. We tell ourselves and others that God is here and He hears.

This is the message we give whether we are in the city or in the village. In turn, He acts and removes my unbelief.

[Chapter 51] Mystery of Christ

/Angela/ I remember my response the first time Joe, our earnest young worship leader, led the congregation in Shanghai, in this chorus:

"We're giving it all away, away. / We are giving it all to go your way."   *Go* Hillsong United

This song is loud, honest and intense. There is something in the way Joe leads it, sings it. "Is this possible?" I find myself asking. Can it be my true, authentic personal anthem as well? This isn't just a song but an invitation to know the Holy.

Will I mean it? Will I give it ... away? Give it all away to go His way?

It was difficult to sing it that night.

Here I was, thousands of miles from our previous home, a family of four with 9 suitcases to our name. What does it mean to give even more away? Haven't I given enough? Oh Lord, you know I have.

The funny thing is, I could go further. Give more away. Not alone, though.

With Jesus on the Cross, ne as my example, I can. I have been reading the Old Testament lately and it is clear that God's chosen people are not free of the snares of sins. Far from it.

If you see extraordinary goodness, it really is the work of Christ. Stay around and observe, we really are all fallen, like angels from the sky. Each wonderfully made like stars above but really hollow like balls of fire until a divine purpose is understood and pursued. Hang out longer and you might even notice some Buddhists or Hindus are acting more spiritual than many Christians.

Try reading the Bible. God's people are wicked, capable of as much sin as any who do not know Him. Fathers eat their children in misguided desperation. Children in turn eat their parents (Ezekiel 5:10). That is what loss of holy vision and intense starvation can do to people. We lose all sanity and become ravaging beasts.

Coincidentally, several weeks before our trip into rural China, we watched the movie "Gandhi" as a family. Here was a man who loved his people, and in order to serve them, he felt he needed to travel and see India.

Like Jesus, Gandhi went to the people. He needed to see how the people rose, how they toiled, how they sang and slept in all their squalor, to see their homes and how they lived their simple lives. In the same fashion, our Lord sat and lived with common folk. Gandhi said, "I like your Christ, I do not like your Christians. Your Christians are so unlike your Christ."

In April, we had a chance to participate in a mission trip to remote Anhui province. We felt led to be the hands and feet of Jesus with strangers. We pulled our boys out of school for a few days to join a group of Christians and delivered livestock and grains to some of the poorer rural folks in Anhui.

I wanted to know China and although the Great Wall seemed an obvious entry on the bucket list, little known Anhui, as my Jesus decides, was my first departure town after months in Shanghai. So I went to this village I have never heard of (and still do not know the name) because I was sure it was the right thing to do.

The very bumpy bus ride through the countryside felt more like a Noah's ark ride on a big endless ocean of wheat fields sprouting up from the good earth. Gorgeous yellow rape flowers filled the countryside landscape mile after mile. The bus was small. My butt hurt from all that bumping around. So long and rough was the ride that it made the train ride from Hefei back into Shanghai a dream. Even the smell of cigarette smoke became a non-issue for me when I finally returned back to the city.

It wasn't the living conditons that bothered me. After all, I had seen pictures of such spartan conditions from pictures my mom took from her own trips into the Chinese countryside. It was what it was. People who live in rural China don't have much. Yet, things are better today than they were a generation ago. It is hard to imagine.

So if you asked what bothered me most, it was being struck once more by the revelation that there really are many needy people out there. Is this what Jesus meant when He said that His fcllowers would "do even greater things" than Him? (John 14:12)

In China, poverty wears a different face. Instead of loneliness and depression that so prevail in America, this country sees a greater disparity in wealth distribution. With potholed dirt roads bearing no names, a local guide is needed to take you around. There is still much to be developed. Poverty abounds and the young are hungry for something bigger. Actually, not very different from the scrubbed up kids of American suburbia.

The children in this rural village that we visited clamored for whatever things our group could bring in our backpacks. Craft supplies were quickly grabbed

199

away from my palm, like how most kids back home grab the latest version of a video game.

I feel both helpless and frustrated. Their hunger for something new and novel is so strong. But *stuff*, as we know, does not satisfy. So what do we give?

We tell them the story of Jesus, the One whose living waters do not run dry.

"This one needs to hear about the Lord. That one there and this one too," a local Christian sister starts grabbing kids and brings them toward us. They come from the left and right, in front of us and from the back, on the second floor of an unfinished church building standing in the middle of wheat fields.

Obedience to the Cross has only one final destination, it seems: to know God's heart. A crowd of lively children in mismatched clothes and dirty mud-stained fingers gathers. With our iPad and Bible picture book open, we tell the story.

"In the beginning, God created the heavens and the earth." We go through the Bible stories so many of us heard in Sunday school and classes. We pass them on. They listened, enraptured.

We tell them about Christ, the Son of God who came and died for us. About His birth, His time on earth and His death on the Cross. We tell the story of His incredible resurrection and the Good News He brings. We tell the story as others before have told us. We tell God's story all in one sitting because deep inside, we know our journey might not return this way again. In other words, we want to give it all away, to go His way for these children.

"Now, lead them to confess belief in Jesus!" the local sister urged. Ron and I squirmed with discomfort inside and were taken aback by her audacious request. Our western minds found it hard to compute that request.

Wait, what about a beginner's class? Aren't you aware they need more grounding? Too bad our Chinese was painfully limited. So, we submitted and prayed for the kids.

"Will you claim Jesus as your Lord?" Ron asked with his gentle voice, a radiance about him.

"Yes," they all said. We gulped.

We looked at them. They are young and wide-eyed, and we are so moved by their open hearts. CEOs and presidents work hard with a staff of people to hone messages that can rouse hearts to their cause. Over here, we are struck by the power of the Spirit. We witness God's glory at work when doubt leaves the heart.

Jesus said, "Let the little children come to me, and do not hinder them, for the kingdom of heaven belongs to such as these." Matthew 19:14

Maybe they *do* understand. After all, if my Bible correspondence teacher, Irene, had ruled me out at the tender age of 14, would I be where I am? She faithfully knocked on my door with her husband and took time to visit me. What about Charlie, my first pastor? Did he know all that time he spent listening and answering my theological questions without judgment, steering me always back to the Bible, would only spur me to do likewise later on?

We have no right to judge the situation here. The Spirit guides. We follow. Ron leads a prayer, telling Jesus we are ready to let him be the Lord of our lives.

I probably would be chided by some for my naïveté.

So be it. I am ready for a China changed by Christ's love.

"Come," he (Jesus) said, "and you will see." John 1:39

[Chapter 52] The Church Builds

/Angela/ "We do things different from American churches," the Chinese church planting couple tell us. "When the money is tight, we don't ask our congregation to give us more. We tell our congregations and our seminary students to fast and pray and we all eat cheaper foods."

This couple is not short of knowing people who have a lot of money. "We fast whenever we want to do something first," both of them tell us. "And we pray. In fact, we do that for days until we get an answer." As we listen to their stories, we realize that this is how they teach their people. Their seminary, with 4,000 students on the wait list, is training leaders for the Chinese church and for mission efforts abroad.

I have witnessed a few of their graduates in action. Many are young, in their twenties and yet they were not only thoroughly grounded in the Word but they carry a deep sincerity in doing the Lord's work. One inspired me to read the Bible more myself, and where did I find her? Like young Timothy in the Bible, she was leading a Chinese 妈咪小组 (mommy's group) where a number of them were older than her.

Another young leader led a long (by my western standards) prayer meeting that kept the fires burning bright. Still another sang with continuous tears during a praise and worship time. They were an unstoppable lot. Praying for others. Getting the concerns of others. Leading others to draw closer to God by their example. Even my mother, who has seen much of the world, was touched by their sincerity and returned to join them many more times on her own after we introduced them to her.

203

Because the Chinese government does not allow meetings beyond a certain size or in non-registered meeting places, the house church structure is how they grow. They meet in numerous sites. Their efforts to be the hands and feet of God are not small in size or intensity at all. When Sichuan had an earthquake, a team was immediately deployed there, with more to follow after reports of what succeeding teams need to bring. When water wells need to be dug in the mountainous regions of Yunnan, several teams are coordinated across the country to make that happen.

They have no multi-pronged giving strategy. No envelopes given out to me as I am greeted at the door of their house church. Nothing is mailed to my home. No easy tithing online, no boxes to check. All I am asked to do is to come pray with them and worship God. And they do it nearly every day, morning and night. They have no youth overnight parties, just monthly all-night prayer meetings. What a really strange, holy church of people!

I read somewhere that one in ten church-going Americans today attends a megachurch. The number is expected to rise in the coming years. The Lord will provide and help us complete our building projects. He will bring in the resources. The people will come. Our targets will be met and sometimes even more. We will be amazed at what God's people can do. In the meantime, we just worship God.

I have seen what ordinary people can do when they are all in. "Just take the money," the people insist. "We trust you completely." Because the evidence is so clear. You really do live out loud for others. For Christ. There won't be any need to use verses from Malachi to remind them why they should open their wallets. Just worship God.

See how Ezra does it? He reads the Law from daybreak till noon, the Bible says. I am not sure what happened there but the people could not stop weeping when they listened to the words of the Law. (Nehemiah 8)

Just what kind of a priesthood is it? Ezra reads and the people weep. The Levites instruct and the people understand.

There was an old man in that village that had some sort of difficulty getting around Ron had prayed a prayer of salvation over that household after they said they were ready to surrender to Christ. It was a very humble home in the countryside. They had a precious porcelain Guan Yin idol in a corner of their two-room home. We knew it presented a potential stumbling block after he said yes to Christ. We asked that man's permission to remove his idol from his home.

Another brother in Christ, a manufacturing manager based in Shanghai, took it once the new believer agreed to let it go. The brother smashed it right outside the house. Our boys who were there to witness it all let out a squeal of delight.

The old man said he couldn't go to church before because his legs were not strong enough. But God just kept calling. When he knelt in prayer to the Lord, his white haired wife also followed and knelt. Both went down on their knobby knees, and the prayers went up.

The group of us who were on this mission trip fell on our own knees as well with them. Suddenly all the fancy job titles or educational status we all carried seemed so embarrassingly small. The Holy Spirit ruled and united all our hearts that moment.

The next day, we found him and his wife attending church for the first time. Across the fields, we saw an old couple make their way to an incomplete building. The man who said he couldn't come, came and showed us that there really was never a time too late to return to the Cross.

[Chapter 53] The House Church

\Ron\ "Let's go worship with the local Christians," I suggested to the family. So we headed out the door on foot, not sure if we would find the place or if we did, what we would find there. But we went and on a holiday weekend we found a small band of believers worshipping intently in the heart of the financial district of Shanghai.

The group was small, maybe 15 people. After settling down and getting the boys in place, I start to relax and also pray, to raise hands and join the saints in singing, in praying and in worshipping God.

Everyone singing was on their knees, kneeling on thick rubber pads. The song is a familiar tune but with Chinese words. The singing is passionate, the exhortations are sincere and heartfelt. The responses by the congregation show engagement, even at the end of this working day (Sundays can become a regular working day in China's crazy holiday schedule). I don't know if this is a thin crowd or normal. I am a little self-conscious as both a newcomer and as the only one in this crowd without any Chinese blood in me. Do I even belong here? There's no translation; it's all in Chinese.

软弱的我变刚强，贫穷的我变富足

瞎眼的我能看见主，给我行了神迹

和散那，和散那，主是被杀的羔羊

和散那，和散那，主是从死里复活

Let the weak say I've become strong,

Let the poor say I am rich

Let the blind say I can see,

It's the Lord's mark on me
Hosanna, Hosanna, to the Lamb that was slain
Hosanna, Hosanna, the Lord died and rose again

给我一颗中国心，一颗中国心

每当我在寄居地歌唱，想到你就哭了

中国啊，中国啊，我心所爱愿你不再哭泣

中国啊，中国啊，若我忘记你

情愿右手忘记技巧，

中国啊，中国啊，若不纪念你

情愿舌头贴于上膛。

Give me a heart for China
Every time I sing and think of you I'm brought to tears
O China! My heart's desire is for you not to cry again
O China! If I forget you, let my right hand forget its skill
O China! If I forget you, let my tongue stick to the roof of my mouth

We stay on the same song, the same verses, longer than I am used to. I look around at the crowd: A lot of younger adults it seems. But there is no rush, and the leaders want us to savor this worship, to use it to come in close to God. So I submit, and also open my heart.

After we have sung for some time, we divide into small groups for prayer. I hear the concerns of En and Deng before we pray for each other, asking for stronger family relationships and for strength to minister, for patience in raising godly children.

After the small group prayer, we have more singing and praise. Angela feels led to share something on her heart with the group. It is rare for her to volunteer, but we went to the front and as a family we gave our witness with Angela doing most of the talking and we three guys giving her support.

More young people slip into the room toward the end of the meeting and we sang another song, this one of blessing for each other.

We saw the pastor's Chinese wife at the end of the service and she came over to greet us and to say she had been praying for us. There is earnestness and sincerity in what is shared here. It is as if we may not see each other again, but if we don't we are not anxious because we are assured of another meeting under much better circumstances.

These people pray and sing in a different heart language from us. They also love their country sincerely and long for the salvation of many. They welcome us as foreigners in their midst, but they don't expect us to do the work for them or to lend finances or anything else. Our presence here and faith is enough for them, and they appreciate that we can share the fellowship and make common cause.

I go away certain that this is the future of China. These young people carry this nation in their heart. They long for their family members who are not believers to embrace the gospel and experience deliverance. They see the lostness in the masses they rub shoulders with every day. They pray for the salvation of the nations, for those near China and those far away.

In hiddenness, God is preparing the ground and getting ready to do great things in the days ahead. Of this I am sure beyond doubt.

[Chapter 54] Jesus Would Love This Manger!

Then Jesus came to them and said, "All authority in heaven and on earth has been given to me. Therefore go and make disciples of all nations, baptizing them in the name of the Father and of the Son and of the Holy Spirit, and teaching them to obey everything I have commanded you. And surely I am with you always, to the very end of the age."
Matthew 28:18-20

/Angela/ "Someone gave us a chicken," Steven announced.

I did not know what to say. I did what I do when I am at a loss for words. I do not speak.

"We are going to try to figure a way to kill it," he continued.

Steven and Paula* (not their real names), urban dwellers from birth, were as baffled as I with this unusual gift. The giver, a country farmer, would know what to do, but not these Christian friends we just met.   I smiled sheepishly and said I wouldn't know either and then proceeded to explore the ancient town by foot with their daughter as our guide.

It is evident that the locals here appreciate this couple living in their midst. This sweet family along with their dog "Lottie" had moved to this ancient town more than 800 years old in southwestern China to open a humble inn. Perhaps I put it too simply because their cause and vision is far wider and bigger than that.

They came because they wanted to be God's emissaries in this tourist town filled with animistic spirits.

"We figure people needed a place to stay and it is something we think we can do," Steven's voice carried a great conviction.

"At least we believe that," he paused as he said that, letting those very words borne out of big dreams sink deep into his heart again.

So on their entrance door, the following words proudly greet weary travelers and happy, curious tourists: "God loves the world," it boldly proclaims. "Love is freely given. All guests are warmly welcome."

My translation of it is poor because the meaning is actually deeper. The couplet of 14 simple characters speaks of people who understand the message behind John 3:16 deeply: "For God so loved the world that He gave His One and Only Son, that whoever believes in him shall not perish but have eternal life."

It speaks of a God who cares deeply for his creation and creatures, who loves us so much that no life is inconsequential, and as a testament offers His only Son to die as a sin offering for a holy life.

Steven and Paula get it. On this quiet cobblestoned street of a popular tourist town, several other Christian families also get it and are on the same path as them. Can you imagine? A handful of families on the move, all deciding after much prayer and prompting to move over a thousand miles (2000 km) to this place to open inns, a respte for the tired tourists, who travel rocky roads and great distances just for a taste of Eden on earth.

"To open inns?" I asked.

"Yes, to open inns," Paula recounted the story once more.

Life on earth is tiring. It is full of things that keep us busy. Things and relationships can satisfy, but not enough. So people seek a paradise on earth. Somewhere to get away to. Away from it all. This is where innkeepers like Steven and Paul come in. They provide the sanctuary-like respite and the spirit of Christ to all they encounter.

In this so-called paradise, where ancient spirituality runs deep, a certain kind of ease resides with the local villagers' everyday life. At the market, sun-weathered grandmothers with heavily calloused hands summon momentary smiles at potential customers but resume their stoic expressions when no purchase is made.

The locals, like us Christians everywhere, have a religious pulse in their daily lives. Traditions that matter to each are observed. Over here, ancient mountains are respected with awe. Crystal clean rivers have run for generations and still do. There is an awareness of the holy, even reverence for it but intentional service by others from the outside world? That sort of selfless love is rare.

It is against this backdrop that I meet my fellow brothers and sisters in Christ, who have made this place their place of livelihood and ministry. They remind me that Jesus is not a tract, a short mission trip, or just money sent across the miles.

When Jesus came to earth, he moved in among us. Took on a human body, learned a human language and culture, grew up in a regular family, got caught in the crossfire of a civil unrest between his own people the

Jews and the Romans. The Word came *near* and dwelt among us, and it started next to an inn in a manger.

"We open inns." That is how Steven and Paula make a living here. That is how they plant the Spirit of Christ and shine the light of Jesus there.

[Chapter 55] Every Tribe, Every Tongue

How beautiful on the mountains are the feet of those who bring good news, who proclaim peace, who bring good tidings, who proclaim salvation, who say to Zion, "Your God reigns!" Isaiah 52:7

/Angela and Ron/ We are sauntering along this massive compound called "Yunnan Ethnic Village Culture Park". We are in southwestern China, in the province of Yunnan. It is winter elsewhere in China, but the weather here is not cold and it is pleasant to walk outside.

We are in a theme park of sorts, devoted to showcasing the almost 30 ethnic minorities that live in Yunnan province. China itself has 56 official minorities, though that doesn't quite cover all of them. The Han Chinese dominate China, making up 93% of the population. What the world thinks of as China is the Han culture.

The minorities in China include the Tibetans, the Manchus, the Uyghur ("wee-ger") and many others. Yunnan borders Tibet and Burma and is a particular hotspot of ethnic diversity.

In Kunming, the capital city of Yunnan, we have made our way across town to the Ethnic Cultures theme park. The Cultural Center is touristy. There are endless stalls selling all kinds of trinkets. We aren't anthropologists but we enjoy exploring other cultures, and this is the best we can manage with our family in the limited time we have in Yunnan. How else could we see all 26 ethnic minorities of Yunnan province in so little time?

214

The park is arranged in small mini-villages, some busy and others quiet. People dressed in native costume are in the villages, and the houses and other buildings important to each tribe are replicated.

Our boys get to ride on top of proud horses around a track at the Mongolian village and they have a blast. Many of the hill tribe villages have thatched huts and simple tools and share a strongly communal culture. What we didn't expect to find, though, were further spiritual lessons in the middle of this ethnic theme park.

Since we came in the winter, during the off-season, the park was unusually quiet and even thinly staffed. The good part is we didn't have to contend with crowds as we enjoyed the sprawling grounds with lush semi-tropical plants, bridges over small lakes and endless walking paths.

In the midst of such quiet, we heard songs come across the water. It was the Lahu tribe, one of the few which had a significant number that in decades past had converted to Christ. Their happy singing had us seek it out as we heard strains of "Hallelujah's" repeated several times accompanied by guitar.

We searched for the source of music and found three men singing, praising God with choruses of "Hallelujah". I understood nothing of what they sang but I will never forget their happy faces on that cool Wednesday afternoon, so lit up and caught up in worship for our God. Their singing, full of joy, was testimony that a Great God moved among their midst. Even the tourists, several apparently well-traveled, many not Christians, paused their busy touring and sat down quietly in the courtyard to listen in on their happy singing.

At another village, the tribesmen could not stop smiling the moment we entered their grounds. I looked over behind my shoulder, half expecting something behind me to warrant such warm greeting. But it was at me they were smiling when I first entered their village. What on earth gave them reason to be so happy, I wondered?

I looked at them, their joyful eyes looked back. One went on to move some things away in a wheelbarrow. Another stood in a corner, waiting to answer any questions while I peered inside to look at their mocked up huts.

I stepped outside their replica living quarters, surveyed their "home" setup and noticed suddenly a church replica as part of their tribal village display. I walked briskly toward it, excited and confounded by the structure.

Then it all made sense. The genuine smiles and happiness. "How could we not be happy?" answered one of the tribesmen, "We know the Lord!"

His answer startled me. Did you catch it?

How could we not be happy? We know the Lord.

Is there any deeper healing truth than that?

We learned from the Miao tribesmen that six or seven Christian families more than a century ago went and settled among the Miao people and shared the gospel with them. Many in the tribe believed, delighted at receiving the Word of God.

When I asked a Miao man if he could show me John 3:16 in his language, I became immediately curious about the people who brought such care to their work. Translation work is laborious and the thrill of seeing a completed Bible in final form wasn't always possible. The script, I was to later learn, was called the Pollard script, and invented by a British missionary by the name of Samuel Pollard of the China Inland Mission just for this language group that had no written script previously.

Pollard and his kind rekind ed for me what love of one's fellow man could look like. Instead of petty theological debates and engaging in endless human drama, perhaps we could all work for an end whose good we might never see? The difference was obvious. The tribes that the Christian missionaries brought the Gospel to were different from those who had not experienced the goodness of God.

Oh, the footprints they left behind. We all have life-transforming stories to tell. Some of us will go and some of us will stay. Let's pray that we do not just keep it to ourselves. Pollard did not. It is clearly God's will that every tribe and every tongue has a chance to hear God's good news. What a joy it is to hear *them* praising God in their own language or reading God's Word, regardless of whether they have a crowd watching or not.

[Chapter 56] Immanuel Became Love

/Angela/ On the next to last Sunday before we left Shanghai, our weekly domestic helper, Huang Ayi, presented me with an embroidered gift. "Immanuel Became Love" - the work of painstaking art proclaimed.

It is a huge red cross that she embroidered. Precious time that could have been used for herself or her three children, she spent it on me. In fact, she was racing against the clock to get it done even though she didn't make a big fuss over it.

I do not know quite what to say. I am stunned when she presents it to me. It is like the way I greet the birth of Jesus at Christmas season. I am so deeply appreciative of it but do I get it? Do I really grasp how much He loves me? That He came to die for me, for all of us. Really? It is so easy to miss the reason for His coming.

It has become common among Christians I know in America to bemoan how we have lost sight of the real meaning of Christmas, that it is about the coming of Jesus into our world. There is some truth in that as the Christmas season has become a vehicle for retail promotion and intensive shopping for gift giving.

But He did come, as Huang Ayi acknowledged in her gift for me. It was given in the heat of summer without a whisper of Christmas in the air. The sole occasion was our imminent departure from China.

"I know how important He is to you and so I made you this," she said. I am touched by her generous heart. Inside I ask, 'But would you accept Him?'

It is not the first time Jesus came knocking on her door. "I was a young girl then," she tells me when I sang Psalms 121 out loud in Chinese. I had been in her home province, Anhui, and picked up the song from the local congregation there. She recognized it immediately and it brought her back to the childhood memory of that time.

Her reasons are nowhere different from so many I have heard. I understand, I tell her. God waited so long for me too. For now, I can only pray for her to have a heart that will be open to the next prompting.

For this moment, she is just that. Not ready for such a heavy commitment and she knows it is more than just a lifestyle change. Seeing it through all the way is no easy assignment. I am so proud of her. This simple woman who tells me she does not know much because she isn't educated. The one thing that truly matters, she knows.

I have been so lucky. Oh my goodness. So many followers of Christ have poured and given much good into my life. Not because they had to or must but because they could, and they did.

Christine manages our mail and statements in the US. She scans everything for us weekly in between her own laundry breakdowns and sports practices. She also sends us dollops of love in the form of homemade taco seasoning and real stories of her family life. Of death in the family, of home improvement projects and what it is truly like to help a son navigate through junior high school.

Then there is our friend, Sam, whom I hear from at least once a month for two years. He helps deposit our house rent so that we could continue to make payments

219

on the unsold house back home. If anyone asked me if I know of any real follower of Jesus, I would say "Yes, I do." Sam like Christine did things for us that taught us further what a heart of service meant. Our gratitude for what he did for us is still irreducible to words today.

"This is how we know what true love is: Jesus Christ laid down his life for us. And we ought to lay down our lives for our brothers." 1 John 3:16

I have loved that verse all the way back when I was just a college student. I have tried to pay attention to find out what that really means. I have been blessed by clues all this while, thanks to some amazing examples in my life.

Immanuel became love for me. God took on flesh and showed me great love. Working through others he continues to do so. Working through me, even still his love will show. This is how we proclaim the cross.

Section 6 – What's Next?

[Chapter 57] Year of the Snake

\Ron\ Every twelve years the Chinese traditional calendar brings around the snake, most recently in 2013. Among the Chinese, the snake has a complicated symbolism which is not an exact match with views in the West. I like to understand symbolism and use it as one key to understanding other cultures.

Ancient Chinese myths give the snake special powers, even creative abilities. The deceptiveness and evil intent attributed to snakes seems to be a later development captured in a number of Chinese idioms. Snakes can be intelligent, beguiling and also dangerous, certainly a creature to watch out for!

Snakes (or serpents) also have a complicated relationship with man based on the Bible.

"Now the serpent was more crafty than any of the wild animals the Lord God had made."

"I will put enmity between you [the serpent] and the woman, and between your offspring and hers." Gen 3:1, 15

"The Lord sent venomous snakes among them; they bit the people and many Israelites died." Numbers 21:6

The Lord said to Moses, "Make a snake and put it up on a pole; anyone who is bitten can look at it and live." So Moses made a bronze snake and put it up on a pole. Then when anyone was bitten by a snake and looked at the bronze snake, they lived. Num 21:8-9

"Just as Moses lifted up the snake in the wilderness, so the Son of Man must be lifted up, that everyone who believes may have eternal life in him." John 3:14-15

There is clearly a complex and intertwined history of threat, trouble, and even redemption that involves people and snakes. Yet, God is also there, and when He is the real focus of our fascination, the threat and guile of the serpent loses its power.

As the year began on this part of our journey back to the cross, there was no real foreboding about what would be coming, no ill portents about the year ahead. If anything, there was anticipation as we were finally leaving the cocoon.

Our family had spent a year and a half in China without leaving the country. It was an intense bonding experience for us, both as a family but also between us and our adopted home.

With the coming of the new year we set off to see another part of China, a wilder part in the Southwest filled with tribes and tropical plants, tea and traditions different from the ones we had grown accustomed to. It was a great family experience and God opened our eyes to more people and more work for the kingdom that is still to be done.

After our time in Yunnan we boarded a plane for Singapore, headed "home" for the Chinese New Year holiday to visit family.

Some people say home is where you come from, others home is where the heart is. Home can mean many different things at different seasons in our lives. Singapore is home for Angela, her birthplace, where she grew up, and where her own family still lives.

Thomas Wolfe said you can't go home again, which in some respects is certainly true, just as you can't step into the same river twice. The stream moves on and things change.

Coming from China, we couldn't help but make comparisons between where we had been and where we landed. Singapore was many things for us: more comfortable, cleaner, easier to get around, warmer, relaxing. But one thing stood out for us: it was also harder for us to hear God's voice. Without a doubt, God still speaks and is moving in Singapore, but *we* found it harder to hear. We strained to listen for and see the signs that were so clear to us in China.

What are we here for? What is next for us? What kind of family are we going to be?

Of course God was speaking, in so many more ways than we could pick out at the time. We went to worship with His people in three different faith communities, we picked up different books that took us down new paths, and the theme that kept emerging was "cleanse yourself."

To go back to the cross is a cleansing experience. We must purge the sin and evil, the questionable compromises we have made, the multiple loyalties we have gotten entangled in.

Singapore is a city-state in a tropical setting. It is one of the cleanest cities you'll visit. If you get away from the built up areas it makes it easier to imagine a lush Eden. I had not been in Singapore for three years, and with our recent experiences in China it was certainly evocative.

In this beautiful garden, I am aware that the serpent is there too, along with a warning and a charge to "cleanse yourself." Do not be seduced, don't sleep-walk through this time. There is danger, but deliverance is also possible. We were refreshed after a month in the garden city, and prepared to return back "home" to spring in Shanghai.

This spring in East China is a time of praying and seeking. The land feels less foreign and more navigable; we have learned our way around here. God is leading us. The Lent season also lets us continue the cleansing that began in February. We will celebrate Easter this year at the end of March, in fact on our 20th wedding anniversary.

Marriage is an act of dying too, dying to self and saying yes to your mate. How appropriate to celebrate Passover and Easter and two decades of marriage all within the same weekend. There is deliverance from near-death and a cleansing as we mark Passover. There is a dying to self and submission to God's will on Good Friday. There is celebration of new life, of hope and love triumphing over the darkness and despair on Easter. And there is the marking of a faithfulness, a commitment to honor and to love that is contained in marriage.

The year of the snake is a human invention. The drama of the serpent is age-old and gives us a wider perspective on the choices and moral dilemmas that confront us. Will we choose to believe the lie or the half-truth? Will we look to the cross and allow Christ to instruct us in what true love looks like, how it acts, the power of life over darkness?

Snakes and serpents can be co-opted for evil just as God can redeem them for his deliverance. Man can mistakenly worship the gift itself instead of the Giver. The call to the heart goes out again: Back to the cross. Cleanse yourself. Walk with Me, in my power. This is what life is really about.

225

[Chapter 58] In the Cloud

\Ron\ I'm sitting here next to the woman (Angela) who twenty years ago on this day said "Yes" to me. I listen to a new song that so perfectly captures where we are now…and also where we are heading.

> *Spirit lead me where my trust is without borders.*
> *Let me walk upon the waters*
> *Wherever you would call me.*
> *Take me deeper than my feet could ever wander*
> *And my faith will be made stronger*
> *In the presence of my Savior.*
> *"Oceans" (Where Feet May Fail)* Hillsong United

Several nights ago I picked up a book sitting on my shelf where it had been there for several years, practically unread. But that night, it gave me light and companionship for an hour or two. It is an old English book from the 1400's called *The Cloud of Unknowing*. That is where we seem to be headed—into the cloud of unknowing, up above the cloud of forgetfulness.

"Stay out of the clouds!" I can still hear Tom's voice ringing in my ears. Tom was my flight instructor in 2007 when I was taking lessons. The first step to flying is usually a private pilot's license, and it allows you to fly when you can see where you're going and what's below you. Flying into and through clouds, blind except for instruments, is not allowed unless you get an additional instrument rating. Until you get that rating and some experience using it, you better stay well clear of the clouds or it spells trouble. Disorientation, hurtling blindly through a misty thick fog, usually ends very badly for pilots inexperienced in handling it.

The writer of *The Cloud of Unknowing* does his best to warn the reader away from the book. "Only read this if you are experienced in the faith, if you are totally, truly committed to loving God with all your heart and you're ready to take the next step." The next step he is talking about is into the cloud of unknowing, not a place for spiritual novices apparently. But that is exactly where I find myself now. It is mostly scary, with some foreboding and only a little exciting.

I can relate to Jesus' disciples, specifically Peter, James and John who went up on a mountain with him and saw him change before their eyes. Dazzling white clothes and the appearance of two great Jewish figures, Moses and Elijah, who embody the Law and the Prophets ....

A cloud wrapped around them, obscuring the vision. In its place, a voice: "This is my Son, whom I love. Listen to him!"

I've been living in Shanghai two years. I've learned to get around the city and around the business world, the market place where I talk to company leaders and managers and gain an understanding of their concerns. I've learned to direct taxi drivers on the best routes and when to avoid taxis and take the subway, how to get a bicycle fixed when the pedal fell off, how to live more in community and less like an isolated American.

I've seen China from a very different perspective than those books I read before I came and the media reports that were easy to believe. Now those things seem superficial and partial. What is really going on here is something different from the news and the official version of events.

I have gained a new way of seeing, a way of walking more in faith and less by sight, of listening to the spirit instead of insisting on what my brain tells me is so.

Don't be afraid to go into the cloud if it is Jesus who leads you there. It may not make sense, and there will be opposition at some point. This journey into the cloud of unknowing requires faith in God and a willingness to take a series of steps, one after another after still another. The cross makes it all possible.

[Chapter 59] Fifteen Minutes or All of Eternal?

/Angela/ So, Andy's in town. The exhibit of Andy Warhol's work this time is called "15 Minutes Eternal". It seems appropriate. Warhol supposedly coined the expression "In the future, everyone will be world-famous for 15 minutes". Andy died in 1987, but his 15 minutes has stretched a little longer than most celebrities.

You look at the exhibit and you see, really, it doesn't take much to create a little fame. Just plain simple drive. With today's rise of social media, the rise to such fame is even quicker.

In contrast, I am thinking about the young people we met this same morning. Their ears and hearts were so open to be fed by the Spirit, and this was possible because the pastor responsible for this flock really schooled them deeply in prayer.

Ron was a guest teacher there today. At the end of John 3, he led a prayer. Lord, we confess our sins. Expecting reverent silence, the people broke into individual confessions.

They were listening and hungering for something deeper. These nameless people—will they get their 15 minutes? It seems like a trivial question.

Among the house churches in China I am often struck by their sincere prayers. I have heard Chinese spoken from a very young age starting in my own home. In the schools I attended in Singapore, I received several hours of Chinese language instruction each week. In other words, I am fluent in the language.

But in China, I am learning my mother tongue anew through the way the Chinese farmers lift their hearts to the great Yahweh; through the heart-breaking cries of the young Christians, their reverent words, their sweet adorations, their moans, their confessions. They make pleas for themselves, for their people, for their country, for the world.

In a language I knew so well I finally hear a beauty that I never knew was possible. No Ph.D. required, nor even a bagful of extensive world travels. Just a strong heart, a stout heart full of belief that God hears.

Their prayers in Chinese move my heart and ears. They make me see the art God creates in the Chinese language, in fact in any language that is used to lift Him up.

This is what happens when people pursue the timeless Eternal. It is art by the ordinary. Art that takes your breath away, that leaves you asking: Who is this Eternal? Certainly not just a mere 15 minutes of personal fame in history.

[Chapter 60] Our Home is Heaven

\Ron\ It is hard now to say when exactly the word came. In Christian circles we talk about God opening doors and closing others. I can look back now and see the doors a little more clearly than I did at the time. What I can say for certain is that the word came to me in a whisper, "It's time to go to the US."

The previous year my Dad had a major surgery on his back. He almost didn't make it back from the operation and recovery. I wanted to go back and see my Dad. There were other circumstances that made it logical for us to plan a trip back to the US. Yet, beyond the circumstances there was a deeper sense that we needed to take our next step of faith and let God lead us to where he could use us next.

There was much that was uncertain. Where would we live? What would we do about our boys and their schooling? Should we plan a return to China or Asia in the near future? What about our livelihood? Then, taking a step in faith and asking God to honor what we were offering to Him, we moved in the cloud of unknowing.

What was really happening was a deeper realization of what it means to go back to the cross. We give up our smug certainty, our need to have the plan and means all worked out in advance. We have to walk obediently even if not fully understanding. The cross calls for humility, for us to walk humbly with God.

The idea of this book came into clearer focus for me, and the possibility of sharing our journey of faith with others was impressed on me as well. We started looking for how to make the journey home. We didn't have the finances. We had airline miles, though, and yet no tickets were available for the whole summer. None.

Then, an opening came at the end of the summer: we could get four business class tickets back to the US even though it emptied my frequent flyer account. Besides not having to pay for the tickets, it would get us back on my Dad's birthday. The timing of the trip and how we would travel really spoke to me that it was in God's hands.

Living "back to the cross" could not just be a momentary, peak experience for us, or something that we had for a short time while in China. It had to be the new normal; otherwise it wouldn't really be following Jesus in the way of the cross.

/Angela/ Sometimes in our moments of self-pity and indulgence, a few girlfriends and I would talk about the things we miss back home and the things we would do when we have the chance to finally go home.

Now that I am finally going home, I find with great surprise that I have many feelings of unease. How could it be? It doesn't matter if I am returning to my home of origin, Singapore, or the United States, a place I've called home for 16 years. The spirit of unease is there. As much as my girlfriends and I long for home, the home nests and lifestyles we have taken years to build, we know it won't be quite the same when we return.

The gnawing feeling that this is not our final place will keep coming back, no matter how happy and content we have created our homes to be.

"Oh, this is heaven!" I once exclaimed out loud after viewing several pieces of great art in succession.

My second son, always with a quick response, quipped, "Mom, there's no such thing as heaven as long as you are on earth!"

I tend to forget this. Especially when things are going good for me, for us, I forget that there is a big wide world out there, that many are lost and hurting without Jesus.

In China, some things grow at a feverish pace. Like buildings for instance. Roads, infrastructure for transport and commerce. The breakneck speed of development is amazing.

Some things, however, are slow to change. Like peoples' habits, thinking. The Chinese are not unique in this. I am also thinking about my own habits, my beliefs and way of thinking.

When I first came, I was often taken aback by laundry hanging out in busy streets. Now, I am thinking, "Pretty in pink. Someone likes pink sheets like I do." Some prejudices though take a longer time to dissolve. Compassion has so much room to fill in my heart still.

There is a phrase in China that explains and gives grace to all the chaos and uneven development here. Foreigners from more developed places often complain that people or ways here are backward. The Chinese say, "还没成熟". Things are not ripe yet, literally it means, "still growing into its fullness". I take it as more than a euphemism. It is confession: things are not great yet, they still need time to ripen.

Isn't that me? Isn't that us, Christians? This is the story of our lives here on earth. This world is not our home, we sing, but we forget and we live like it is. We accumulate stuff and hang on to it, plan life goals and then work uncompromisingly to make them happen, sometimes even to the detriment of important relationships.

Will we remember the transience of it all, like our time in Shanghai, that this life we live, whether it is rich or poor, happy or sad, that it really is also temporary? The assignment is really to go home, to go home into the safe arms our Savior, and to bring as many along as we can. Don't make the trip heavenward alone—bring others with you!

[Chapter 61] Bold New Dreams

/Angela/   What a full week we have had this holiday week.

In China, several major holidays are based on the old lunar calendar, so they don't fall on the same date each year. The government also offsets some days off with work days, and these may in fact fall on a weekend.

My younger son, who enjoys a good holiday, was disheartened and confused about why he had to attend school on a Saturday, a Sunday or both at times. Once, at his local school, the kids had an extra day off for a particular holiday but they had to do seven days in a row of school the following week without a break to make up for the "lost" day.

"It is a funny way to give a break when they have to make up for it," said my younger son, not concealing some annoyance. But such is China, who has her own rules and rhythms often incomprehensible to others outside.

We went along with an extra school day on Saturday, but we bucked the system and decided to hold the boys out of school on Christmas Day (not a public holiday in China). There was an impromptu gathering at our church on Christmas morning at 10am so we went to join it.

"I am so glad you went over and said 'hello'," I complimented my Singaporean friend, Jo. She has a heart for China and I admire her ease at making connections with the locals here. She had just greeted a local family who were new visitors. "I bet they are glad to meet you!" I continued.

At the end of the service, Jo's eyes went to the back of the church and that was where she made contact and greeted the family of three: a father, a mother and their beautiful young daughter.

It turned out these local Chinese guests at our special Christmas service shared a common friend with Jo. Immediately the family of three relaxed that we were not entirely strangers to them. It was a small crowd that day. Most expatriates were gone from the city and home for their Christmas breaks.

"I think the Lord arranged for them to meet *you*!" she said to me.

Excuse me? Jo, who always has an easy way of handing hard truths to others, dishes another one to me.

After the introductions, it turned out that this couple was on a quest to learn more about Christian homeschooling. And it so happened that we have a little experience with that. They were all ears to hear more.

I weighed what Jo said. Eventually we invited the family over to our home. Again, after all the sharing about homeschooling, we found out their story had much more to it than you would have guessed at first.

They had experienced betrayal, innocence lost and a marriage on the brink of collapse. But they shared about their conversion to Christ in the past year and the healing that was still taking place.

"Had this friend of ours not left us a Bible, I doubt we would have saved our marriage." In a country where mistresses are often tolerated and "innocent" flings are common, but where divorces are also on the rise, our friends opted for a lifeline for their marriage and a new life dedicated to God.

On one particular Labor Day holiday, we managed to find ourselves in a suburb of Shanghai with these Chinese friends. We had been journeying with this Chinese family, and that day was a moment from all our hurried and busy schedules to see all their aspirations in a concrete form.

How amazing it is when God's people envision new dreams and possibilities. Understanding local politics, they were able to successfully partner with a local government authority to secure a strip of shops for their homeschooling community. But their dreams extend beyond people like themselves; they also see it as a place that could provide many useful services for the community at large.

It is exciting to hear their dreams. Broken people who say they do not wish to be broken anymore but want to be used by God. There is something exciting that happens when one actively wants to be changed by Christ at the foot of His Cross. We keep giving Him our sins in exchange for new beginnings. The camaraderie among them, their desire to live closely with one another and sharing everything gave us an idea what an Acts 2 community might look like.

In contrast, on the other side of Shanghai, we visited a school using curricula that blended from the best of Western and Chinese classical traditions. The receptionist who greeted us was a young woman, and her child was a student there.

"Why put your child here?" I asked her.

"Because it is safe here," she told me. It did make sense. If I was a single mom, I would want my child placed in a safe, Christian pre-K school too.

Contrary to some of our misinformed beliefs, the authorities have not blocked all Bible content like stories of Moses and Joseph. In fact, at the 7 story Shanghai Bookstore on Fuzhou Lu, one can easily find story books and audiobooks about characters from the Bible. But they do not tolerate anyone who brings dissonance. Come to China. Bring your knowledge, bring your skills, not your prejudice or fear. Most of all bring your love for the people here. They certainly welcome you for that.

[Chapter 62] Back to Jerusalem

"I will bring them back to live in Jerusalem; they will be my people, and I will be faithful and righteous to them as their God." Zechariah 8:8

\Ron\ One thing I have learned from some Christian believers in China is their passion for mission. In the most populous nation on earth that is probably less than 10% Christian, the people who believe in Christ here have set their hearts on a stunning mission movement that they have called "Back to Jerusalem".

There was a handful of Chinese Christians in the 1930's and 1940's who received a call to head west into the dry high desert regions in China's west to evangelize among the Muslims, Buddhists and others, and then beyond China into Hindu lands, Central Asia, the Middle East and to trace the Silk Road itself back to Jerusalem. This mission movement was stalled before it could even take off due to the Communists coming to power in China in 1949 and closing its borders.

Many outsiders believed the church all but died in China over the next 30 years as all foreign missionaries were expelled, church buildings were closed and Christians were actively persecuted. Mao's wife Jiang Qing declared, "Christianity in China has been confined to the history section of museums. It is dead and buried."

But something else happened. As Christians were driven underground, as worship was stripped to its bare essentials, the refining fire of opposition forged faith that was tested by the most difficult circumstances.

Chinese believers emerged from these dark days more fervent in their faith and changed by the experience. Today they know they can face extreme hardship, prison, persecution and death, and the gates of Hell will not prevail against the church of Christ. What better training for taking the gospel into the non-Christian peoples of Central Asia and the Middle East in fulfillment of a full-circle trip of the gospel from Jerusalem to the ends of the world and back. What is so special about Jerusalem? Let's stop and think about it.

The site of Mount Moriah, where Abraham was called to sacrifice Isaac. The city of David and center of his kingdom. The site of the temple that Solomon built and the second temple that was raised after a remnant of Jews returned from Babylonian exile. The same Jerusalem that Jews made pilgrimage to three times a year during the feast days. And of course the place where Jesus of Nazareth was crucified and raised back to life after three days. Then seven weeks later and after a time of dedicated prayer and waiting, it also served as the place where his disciples rose up in the power of the Spirit and launched a movement that continues to grow and impact the world.

This is the Jerusalem that Asian Christians are headed back to. The way ahead will be tough and will have much suffering. Until I lived in China, I didn't quite understand the value of having suffering in one's personal or cultural history. But it is precisely the ingredient some of us need to participate in God's call to live the life and fulfill the mission He intends for us.

God doesn't just call us to be grim and serious. There will also be joy and miracles and transformed lives as a growing number of believers turn their hearts back to the cross and set their sights on Jerusalem.

Back to Jerusalem. God's mission is not entrusted to a few select people or nations, or only to Christians from the West. God's mission is sweeping and embracing. It is big enough to take on different expressions when you see it incarnated among different cultures. It is diverse enough to take on individual expression for each person it touches.

Amid all of this diversity and breadth, the Chinese remind us that the word of the Lord has gone out from Jerusalem, and the nations will return to Jerusalem. (Isaiah 2:3, 35:8-10, 44:24-26; Zechariah 8:8, Acts 1:12, 8:25).

[Chapter 63] Closer, Richer, Deeper

So then, just as you received Christ Jesus as Lord, continue to live your lives in him, rooted and built up in him, strengthened in the faith as you were taught, and overflowing with thankfulness. Colossians 2:6

/Angela/ It is Monday, our last day in Shanghai. I am coordinating final details with my landlady. We are arranging a final walkthrough of the apartment before she returns the rental deposit to us. These are some of the last details to take care of before we take our flight out of Pudong headed to the US.

On Saturday evening we said farewell to the Body of Christ at Grace Extended. We were prayed over. They asked for final last words, as they often do for departing expatriates out of Shanghai. We mentioned about how our home group came about. Willingness and faithfulness - those were the two words I remember I said. I wish I could give a more inspiring speech but I do not possess such gifts.

On Sunday Ron walked in the pouring rain and preached a sermon to the Chinese congregation. He had an umbrella and still his pants were thoroughly soaked but nobody minded. When I arrived to catch the tail end of his message, they wanted me to share something as well.

I did what I always seem to do. My eyes went big and I said, "Me?" Amos, the prophet in the Old Testament often comes to mind.

I was neither a prophet nor the son of a prophet, but I was a shepherd, and I also took care of sycamore-fig trees. But the Lord took me from tending the flock and said to me, 'Go, prophesy to my people Israel.'" Amos 7:14-15.

I went forward and spoke. The room was full of Chinese people, some young, several old. Then it happened again. I was needed to confess my truth for someone there. It was true for me, but several there needed to hear it spoken by someone else who was unafraid to confess. As I spoke with ease about an unpleasant truth, my translator broke into heavy emotions. Another from the congregation called out, "Continue, sister!" in Chinese. I left that gathering in awe once more how big His Kingdom is.

Shi Ayi called me on the final day in Shanghai. I finally connected with her after my alone time by the Huangpu River. God is the Great Restorer.

"嗨! 时阿姨，你好！" (Hi there, Shi Ayi!)

"I am going to so miss you," she said in a wistful voice. She is my mother's age but we seem to get each other like girlfriends. But because she is older and willing, she is wiser in many other ways that my current age and circumstances don't allow me to be.

We exchanged a few words that departures often call for. Then out of the blue, she started crying and tells me the hurts and misunderstandings she had to bear from her siblings. These are al older folks and my mind said: Is that how it goes? As we age, we wake up one day, full of hurt, unforgiveness and pain?

In that moment, I saw my destiny once more. To be a messenger of hope and peace. What I give is not enough. My job really is to simply point them back to Jesus, back to the Cross.

Pray for forgiveness, I tell her. And I stop myself. Because I know. It *is* hard. It takes something out of us to love someone who doesn't or won't love us back.

I found the only possible way to do superhuman things, to accomplish what seems like impossible tasks, is through the help of God in me. He gives me strength. He gives me the love to do so.

When the landlady and her shifty assistant asked for the copies of some of the apartment leasing papers back, I am puzzled but ask no questions. She plonks down a hefty stack of 100 RMB bills on the dining table. It's a couple thousand US dollars. We are supposed to count it to see if the money is correct. But I am distracted. I look at her cute pink Christian Dior bag (yes, the real deal). Suddenly I realize expensive bags do not just carry lipstick and a purse but sometimes also huge heaps of rental deposit money as well.

In China, there are electronic payments and bank transfers, but common people don't use them for things like this. Most people prefer deals done verbally and simply with plain cash. It is a strange system to me but this is China.

This causes me to realize something in the moment. We think the car, the house, the bank accounts or the title might do the trick and give us happiness. But in the end only a relentless pursuit to do and live His will truly "does the trick". Everything else eventually feels phony, empty, just not quite enough.

We came to learn fluent Chinese, to work, and be a light for Jesus. Our mission bears no great strategy. In short, we learn to witness God's miracles at work and simply believe again the beauty and truth behind the Cross. It applies even in Communist China.

We all hurt. We all have done wrong. We all seek forgiveness from someone or the other. And we all seem to desire peace, love and joy.

At least, that is what I have come to find, as I walk myself back to the Cross. Even close friends and intimate family cannot replace a relationship with God. It is not an easy path. I do not recommend it for the dabbler, the fan or faint-hearted. This is the path of a "long obedience in the same direction" as Eugene Peterson puts it, echoing Nietzsche of all people.

Twenty-five years after that first "yes", here I am. I find myself still wanting to follow Him. I went to Shanghai, confirmed by a call in a dream, yet convinced that it was my husband and my kids who need this experience more than I. Yet, the Lord is gracious. He does not forget me. He desired that I too waste no time here. In turn, because I was willing, I found myself led back to the Cross, closer, richer and deeper.

His mercy truly overflows. And I am still learning to wrap my head and heart around that.

[Chapter 64] Landing

"Jesus replied, "Go back and report to John what you hear and see: The blind receive sight, the lame walk, those who have leprosy are cured, the deaf hear, the dead are raised, and the good news is preached to the poor. Blessed is the man who does not fall away on account of me." Matthew 11:4-6

/Angela/ So Catherina thought I was her Godsend. I think it ran both ways. After a nonstop fourteen hour flight, we are back in America- the land of the big, wide and plenty.

"I didn't have to serve you, you know," she later told me, "I work the Qantas desk but something made me."

It was 11 pm. We had just flown in from Shanghai Pudong International Airport to Los Angeles.

"I know," I responded. I do not need security cameras to tell me when people wish to ignore me. "But I am glad you did," I continued.

"Boy, am I glad I did!" she spoke with an intensity that summoned my attention completely. "You are like an angel sent from God." Instantaneously, my jet-legged self awoke.

I paused to ground myself that moment. God is here even as we changed time zones and read signs in English again. Caterina and I took pictures to remember our encounter.

I gave her my only leather bound Bible, the one with our last name in gold letters on the brown cover. It was so pretty and I took pride in owning it. "Did I really just do that?" I ask myself again. Yes, I did.

It wasn't because I knew the words between the pages by heart. Nor was it because I have no need for it. In fact, I quite like this Eugene Peterson's translation of the Bible. So, why did I give it away?

I just had to. The Word is meant to be lived out, not stored away or held tightly and possessively. When we give it away freely, then we get more of it.

"I can smell the sea, mommy!" Titus yelled in excitement. Yes, our younger son had especially missed America and I would have a small fortune if I could bottle all that happiness in him.

We all took in a deep breath and let out a sigh of great relief after all 12 pieces of our luggage were retagged for the domestic flights. Two more connections and we're home.

Titus was right. The air in L.A. that evening was cool and we did smell the sea. On the other side of that big ocean lies China, the place we just left that so many thought was a great adventure for us. It certainly didn't feel that way when Titus got swiped by an electric scooter and then the culprit just took off. Neither was it fun when the ATM machine issued a receipt that I made a withdrawal and yet no cash came out

It was good to be back on American soil. It felt solid. Yet our hearts knew that over there, where the sea of people is in frantic motion and where the air is often smoggy, God walked with us like a protective wall of fire and a strong cloud of safety above our heads.

God, will you walk with us here too? In this land of milk and honey? We remember several years ago when we were last on this shore. It was complacency and

247

ease that muffled your voice in our ears. It was full stomachs that dulled the appetite for true spiritual food.

A couple of months after we landed softly and easily back home, we found ourselves house hunting. At one particular sales office for a home builder, we met a beautiful blonde woman. "I like this church I attend because I don't feel judged there. I can just go, worship God and then head home," she says. Her honesty got my attention. We had just visited that church ourselves.

After a divorce and while raising two young girls, the least she wanted was to be friendly to "Sunday strangers", or to endure the second-guessing of people who might suggest she should have tried harder in her marriage. I wouldn't want to talk to anyone either when my world is spinning faster than I can manage. Meeting her was no mere circumstance. It was as if God was saying, "Remember this. This land of honey and plenty has many hurting people and I need you here."

But how? People live behind gated communities, many have dogs as their closest daily companions, and social media seems like enough human interaction for so many staring endlessly into their screens. How do you build bridges with other humans in real-time when people keep themselves safe and inaccessible behind all kinds of walls? God, please provide an answer.

[Chapter 65] Greater Glory

"..the Counselor, the very Holy Spirit which the Father will send in my own name will teach you the meaning of all things I have said, and he will remind you of everything I have said to you. I leave my peace with you and I will give you the wholeness, not as the world gives (and takes away). Don't be upset and anxious about this"   *John 14:26-27, (my translation) also 14:12, 16*

\Ron\ As I mentioned before, it is uncommon to see a cross in public in China. Despite the fact that Christianity was introduced here at least as early as 630 AD and has had several periods of widespread recognition, the Christian message or gospel has yet to penetrate and sink roots into Chinese soil. In a land where the cross is so little represented and hardly understood, in this place is where I came to see the need for Christians today to get back to the cross.

Some people do not like to talk too much about the cross. Even among Christians I have found people who don't like too much attention to be given to the blood and tears and sweat, to the flogging, mocking and sufferings of the cross. And yet, this physical suffering is part of the reality of how Jesus was treated in his last hours. It also provides a graphic backdrop for understanding *why* Jesus went to the cross and what it means for us today.

The New Testament writers unflinchingly deal with the cross and its very real sufferings and physical agony. This is remarkable, because in the times when all the gospels and letters were written, the fact that Jesus died on a cross was truly a liability for the Christian faith. Influential Roman citizens, educated and cultured inhabitants of the empire, conscientious Jews throughout the Eastern Mediterranean all would have found a crucified Messiah ridiculous or repulsive.

249

As a symbol, the cross has lost most of these negative connotations in the modern world. It is a symbol of the Christian faith, an identifying mark. It has even, strangely, become a hip sort of fashion icon in the culture apart from religious symbolism. In truth, the meaning and message of the cross has lost its sharpness and distinctive quality amid the media-soaked, data-drunk culture we are living in.

It is not simply a need to understand what the cross means. The greater need and challenge is to return to the claim that the cross makes upon our daily decisions, our choices about what we do with our time and money and talents, the large and small decisions about where we live and what we eat and how we talk and what we value in our deep hearts.

The cross calls us to come and die, certainly. But it is not just about suffering and morbid preoccupation with death. It is also about joy abounding and having your eyes opened to wonder and new discoveries that could only come by choosing to leave behind the familiar and embrace God's *more* for you.

Many people today feel the need for something more than material pursuits and the hollow, plastic lies that are hustled and marketed relentlessly. There is a desire for spirituality, for spiritual depth. What is often missed in the message of the cross today is what Jesus promised his followers soon before his death.

He told them it is *better* for them that he dies on the cross (he called it "lifted up"), for him to go away so that the Father would send the Holy Spirit to live inside us. In a world hungry for spirituality and meaningful spiritual depth, it is certainly good news that God is ready and desirous of giving us his very own Spirit to live inside us, to guide us and comfort and heal and reveal more of who He is for us.

The cross is crazy; it short-circuits our understanding, forces our minds to deal with our hearts and confront our wills. The cross reveals that at the center of existence is a battle between good and evil, life and death, and that love has the final word, not the mind nor the sword. It also makes total demands upon us. Half measures, partial sacrifices will not suffice. Complete commitment is required, total surrender and obedience is the way to freedom.

The cross is liberating and powerful too. It defeats death, renders sin powerless, unleashes the powers of heaven for healing and salvation and service.

"Let us fix our eyes on Jesus...who for the obedience set before him endured the cross and embraced God's joy even in the face of initial suffering and pain." Hebrews 2:9, 14; 12:2

I traveled to China, thinking I was carrying a strong faith with me there. I actually encountered Jesus and the cross there in a more profound way. The way of the cross is about sacrificing the ego and what makes earthly sense so that God's Spirit can teach us something *real*, something truly wonderful and unexpected, something that in the most improbable way is really good news. That is the essence of the cross. It's time to get back to the cross.

"I am waging war for you...that you may really know the mystery of God, which is Christ, in whom are hidden all the treasures of wisdom and knowledge." Colossians 2:2b-3

251

[Chapter 66] What's Next?

\Ron\ This is where we stop *our* story and turn the attention over to you. Where are *you* right now? Do you have the cross in view? Do you have Jesus in sight? Where is God calling you back to the cross?

I recommend you read through Mark's gospel (second book in the New Testament-Bible). It's the shortest of the four books focused on Jesus, but it is action-packed and it has a clear focus.

Pray through Mark and let God lead you on your own journey to the cross and beyond. Spend time focusing your attention on drawing in closer to Jesus. The following words of Jesus give us His invitation and promise.

"Abide in me, stay in me, and I will remain in you. It's just like a branch that cannot bear fruit unless attached to the main vine. None of you can bear fruit unless you abide/stay in me... If you stay in me and my words abide in you, you can ask whatever you want and it will happen." John 15:4,7 (my translation)

I look back now and I can see God certainly answered that prayer. If you pray something fervently that is rooted in God's will and seek to live it out, you will most definitely get what you are asking for.

Earlier in the book, I encouraged you to pray a specific prayer to draw near to God and better grasp the cross. Now as we close I want to return to it.

I ask you to join me again in praying this: "God, I have decided to know nothing except Jesus Christ and him crucified. He is all power and all wisdom. Let me also be crucified with Christ and become like him in his death so I can know him more fully and the power of his rising from death. Let this mystery, the fullness of Jesus' death and rising, be known and experienced in me. Amen."*

Join us on this journey back to the cross and let us together point to what really matters. Share your story with us and read about others who are on this path at www.backtothecrossbook.com

*1 Corinthians 2:2, 22-23; Galatians 2:19, 6:14; Philippians 3:10

45896331R00147

Made in the USA
Charleston, SC
07 September 2015